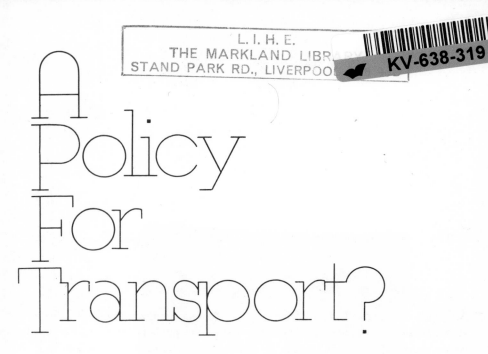

A Policy For Transport?

Papers presented to a conference
at Nuffield Lodge with an introduction
by C D Foster

The Nuffield Foundation

© The Nuffield Foundation 1977

First published in 1977 by the Nuffield Foundation, Nuffield Lodge, Regent's Park, London NW1 4RS

ISBN 0 904956 15 6

Printed by The Blackburn Times Press, Blackburn

Contents

↙ See Below

Definition: Rejoinder
an answer to a question
a retort, a reply!

The papers in this volume were prepared for a conference in 1976 under the chairmanship of Professor Christopher Foster held at Nuffield Lodge on April 8 and 9, shortly before the publication of the Government's Consultation Document on transport. Some papers have been brought up to date in the light of this Document. The views expressed are those of the contributors to the volume and not those of the Trustees of the Foundation.

INTRODUCTION: TRANSPORT POLICY AND RESEARCH
Christopher Foster*

All except one of the papers in this volume are written by authors whose professional occupation is research, many of whom specialise full-time on transport.
As will appear they have a wide range of technical backgrounds – in engineering,
operations research, sociology, planning and economics. They are not shown by
their papers in this book working at the frontiers of knowledge however, but
reflecting on the usefulness of the research they have specialised in. Without
exception what they say is intended to be relevant to transport policy. Indeed
these essays discuss many of the most important and unresolved issues in
transport of the 1970s. As a senior official engaged in transport planning at the
Greater London Council, Alexander Grey writes generally about current
problems and the difficulties of executing policies once decided. Peter Hills
reviews the history of environmental concern as it has built up in transport
planning from the early days of the Wilson Committee and Colin Buchanan. He
discusses how policy and research have responded to this and suggests what we
need to do to improve environmental protection and planning in transport.
Mayer Hillman is particularly interested in the hardship of those who do not
have cars or who are for other reasons put at a disadvantage by the growth of
car ownership and the decline of public transport. Ray Thomas takes a question
which is of great importance to those who plan cities as politicians or local
government officials. So much is going on at the same time in any city. Road
speeds may be falling, but journey lengths increasing. Some services are being
cut while others are being improved. How does one decide overall whether transport conditions in any local area are worsening or improving? How does one
establish whether experiments or such simple matters as fares policies have failed
or succeeded? How does central government decide where conditions are worst
and where central aid is most needed? There are conceptual problems in
deciding what constitutes an improvement, and for whom; but there are also
measurement problems in finding simple enough, yet reliable, indicators of
change. In his contribution, Richard Pryke analyses the performance and
efficiency of the railways; but also widens his argument to maintain that the

* Director, Centre for Environmental Studies

tendency in recent years to subsidise public transport at an increasing rate, however well intentioned, has had unexpected and profound adverse effects. Little of the money has resulted in better public service. Most of it has been absorbed in various forms of inefficiency — in particular over-manning. Pryke also argues that much of the criticism of the motor car under-rates the real benefits it has brought to a very large section of the community. Possibly Colin Buchanan was right in the title of his first book to call the car 'A Mixed Blessing', but the burden of Pryke's argument here is that too many pro-public transport writers now write as if it were an almost unmitigated curse. To which Mayer Hillman and Ann Whalley make a vigorous rejoinder principally in the interests of the pedestrian.

What is the relevance of research in transport to transport policy? There is no difficulty in stating the methodological relationship. A researcher's main job is to establish facts about transport: to explain the past and the present; and to try to predict the future. But it is also legitimate research to use what is known about the past and present to estimate the probable effects of different futures. These might arise by external changes, such as dramatic changes in energy costs or technology, or from changes in transport policy among other things. Over the last twenty years there has been an almost unceasing demand from many diverse and frequently opposed quarters for changes in transport policy. There have been three major Acts of Parliament (1962, 1968 and 1974); and the 1976 Consultative Document again proposes many changes. When there is so much change and talk of change, a major service researchers can provide is indeed to make their best estimates of the factual consequences of such changes. Not however that researchers are usually content only to analyse the implication of policy changes proposed by others. The policies they propose themselves, and those put forward by others which they choose for examination, reveal their political and social values. These are as varied as those of any group of laymen. As has already been said there are differences of view between authors in this book; and the most marked is between Mayer Hillman and Richard Pryke. But they scarcely differ over questions of fact. It is their values that draw them apart.

More interesting than methodology is, I believe, the real influence of research on transport policy and practice; and vice versa, the effect of real events and policy changes on the direction of research.

After the Second World War investment in road and rail was given low priority. The turn of both came at the same time in the mid-fifties when the great Railway Modernisation Plan and the equally great Motorway Network came to be funded. The ambition of the engineers concerned with both was to try to catch up on what had already been done overseas. In this period transport research tended to be technical — more concerned with means than ends. Brilliant research was done on technologies of highway design and construction, on railway signalling and, to some extent, on locomotion. Quite rightly the highway engineers believed that the demand for the roads they were building was buoyant. Common sense and judgement (plus some vehicle counts and origin and destination studies) were enough to tell them where and what they should construct. The railways were equally sure there was latent demand which would justify the railway modernisation they wanted, but they of course were wrong.

Unlike the American highway engineers with almost twenty years from the end of the Second World War before they ran into opposition – or the French railway modernisers who had almost as long though they started later, both the Ministry of Transport road engineers and the Railways were slowed down by strong opposition before the end of the 1950s. There are many engineers – both road and rail – who rue this and regret bitterly that the rate of investment was not kept up even ten more years before it began to decline. To this day they believe that an abundance of first class motorways and railways would have persuaded public opinion that the cost was worth it – despite the very heavy public expenditure that would have been required to finance the roads and meet a railway deficit of French or German proportions. Sorrowful highway engineers tend to look at the United States for the model of a motorway system they believe we would have liked (where of course the railways, or at least the passenger services, have not been modernised). Sorrowful railwaymen have equally looked to France or more recently to Japan (rather than Germany where the railways are not particularly modernised, just expensive and protected) where there has however been relatively much less expenditure on highway construction.

In the 1950s and the 1960s in Britain we were trying to have both modern motorway and railway systems, both very expensive and to some extent competitive. Failure to decide on rational grounds what was the optimal balance between road and rail is the often spoken about problem of transport 'coordination' that was never really tackled.

The early opposition to the Motorway Network modernisation was from the Treasury who were worried about a growth in public expenditure that they had no rational means of controlling. Treasury officials were disturbed both by the growth of transport investment in road and rail and also by growing railway deficits as the expected demand failed to materialise. As might have been expected the Treasury turned to the economists. This coincided with a recent professional interest among the economists in issues relevant to transport – in the estimation and evaluation of social costs and benefits, the choice of discount rates, the proper basis for comparing investments with different investment and pricing criteria and so on. At much the same time there was interest among some mathematicians, engineers and economists in solving some of the mathematical and economic problems involved in representing and modifying the complex networks which are characteristic of transport.

For many years UK research on investment and pricing criteria in transport was as advanced as anywhere in the world. Britain was one of the first countries to face seriously the problem of deciding the balance between private and public transport. Some of the most exacting debate on this was in the context of the Greater London Development Plan. This started as a pure motorway study but was modified to encompass public transport. Economic evaluation was progressively sophisticated. In its various stages, great ingenuity and improvisation went into attempts to try and model the environmental elements, the effects of traffic restraint and a number of other issues that objectors to the Plan thought important. Unfortunately the work was never all pulled together in time. A major research task not yet attempted would be to reconstruct, from the mass of evidence, a method of evaluating complex networks which would have stood the test of the objections made at the time. Although it did not happen in London, evaluation was taken to a fine art elsewhere. In many respects the South East Lancashire, North East Cheshire Transportation Study and the work of the Roskill Commission on the Third London Airport remain models of this approach. It can still be claimed that London Transport and some of the Passenger Transport Executives are world leaders in the application of economics and operations research to their problems. On the highway side of the Department of Transport economic evaluation has been taken as far again as anywhere in the world.

Despite the able researchers working in this field some of the momentum has gone out of this line of research and it is not as clear as it was that Britain is abreast of the best European or American research. The reasons for this are common to the problems of UK research in other fields.

1. Many researchers were more interested in theory and theoretical problem-solving than application. Development requires a large number of researchers applying basic notions to a wide variety of circumstances but few transport problems are quite the same and because the values do vary, considerable ingenuity is often required to apply general principles to particular cases. In the sheer number of researchers in universities and research institutes, the United States have an advantage in that respect.

2. Many who are, in spite of this, most engaged in application and research are inside large organisations – public corporations and central or local government. But the habitual secretiveness of such organisations, in a comparison with similar bodies abroad, means a high proportion of their work is not published, does not fertilise and is not recognised by international scholarship.

3. Most important of all the research task has become more complicated both because public opinion demands that environmental, energy saving and, to some extent, employment effects should be taken into account when

decisions are made and because of a fragmentation of values. Moreover, the consequence of the difficulty of analysing these issues rationally, and the shortage of researchers able to do this, is that an increasing number of questions which are matters of fact and amenable to research are instead decided politically.

Environmental factors

As Peter Hills shows in his paper there has been substantial research into the environmental consequences of transport decisions. Techniques have been developed measuring the most important: noise, air pollution, the effect of vibration on buildings and even what is called visual intrusion. There has also been research on measures to alleviate environmental effects. There are many that could, for example, reduce vehicle noise and pollution. Most difficult of all there have been a number of important attempts to ascribe values to these environmental effects so as to get measures of what the sufferers or beneficiaries would be prepared to pay. Yet, in spite of this, hard information is rarely presented on the environmental consequences of any transport decision. We hear so much of the environmental benefits of transferring traffic from road to rail. There have been a very few incomplete studies of this question but, when there is so much public interest in it, one might have expected a major research exercise which could be a basis for public debate. Much again is made of the environmental impacts of motorways, almost always without benefit of hard information. It was predictable that, if the Channel Tunnel had not been killed on economic grounds, it would have been bitterly fought by environmentalists, yet no environmental studies were commissioned though large sums were spent on traffic studies.

Energy and employment

Precisely the same points can be made as for the environment. The transport consequences of changes in oil prices can be researched. They should bear upon important decisions: the transfer from road to rail, the future planning of our cities and even on the distribution of population. Various small pieces of research have been commissioned but one might have thought by now very substantial work would have been done which would have made it clear on factual grounds what changes in transport policy should be made. There have also been a number of studies of the employment in industrial consequences of transport investments and policies but here again matters which are researchable have to be treated as matters of opinion in much transport decision making. To take one example, the new London River Line may not be justified economically on traffic grounds, or as relieving congestion, or environmentally, or in terms of energy saving, but it is defended on the grounds that it will help bring employment to the East End. There have been a number of studies of the employment-

6

creating effects of somewhat similar transport investments in other countries as well as in Britain. They tend to be patchy and not easy to generalise from. Again one might have thought that when so many millions of pounds were at stake there was a strong case for research to demonstrate whether this underground railway is likely to have the effects predicted.

Income distribution

Before the fragmentation of values, economists had a dodge which was widely accepted. They used to argue that one could ignore the income distribution effects of major changes on the assumption that these could be taken care of by the tax system. Government, it used to be argued, could achieve the income distribution it wanted by altering taxes and therefore did not need to consider the income distribution effects of particular non-tax changes. Thus it could concentrate on the criterion of economic efficiency in relation to such changes. In broad terms, one only had to ask which alternative course of action would most favourably affect Gross National Product. This assumption still has great advantages. If one tries to consider the income distribution effects of a multitude of disconnected actions, the net effect on income distribution of so many changes taking place is hard to calculate. What may appear more trivial but is a serious problem to the researcher, there is also a multiplying of the information needed for rational analysis of issues. However, the research can be done. Much has already been done on such issues as distribution effects of road pricing, traffic restraint, railway subsidies, and the Third London Airport. In practice these analyses tend to be carried out rather late in the course of political argument and not to be deployed so as to influence decisions. Sometimes one thinks it is simply because so much information becomes indigestible that it is seldom regarded by those who take decisions. However, research into systematic and simple ways of estimating the major income distribution effects of transport decisions should help clarify many important issues. In practice many questions about distribution are transmuted into political decisions. It is, of course, a political decision how much weight to give to the interests of, say, the lowest decile in the income distribution but it has not been unknown to argue – for example, against road prices or certain forms of traffic restraint – that a certain course of action is in the interest of the poor, when there are strong reasons to suppose they would not be the beneficiaries.

It is unfortunate that the research requirement is demanding and expensive, though small in cost by comparison with the cost of the investments or policy changes proposed and effected. This is not only because widening the scope of transport research requires more collection and analyses of information but also because it requires careful communication so that it may be appreciated by, say, all the parties to a motorway enquiry. As yet we only have a few 'experimental' examples of what research can do. The major research question in transport is,

I believe, whether we leave it at this and continue to allow so many important decisions to be made irrationally and unscientifically, or turn to a more systematic approach. Perhaps a few studies of major issues — of how the environmental factors affect the division of traffic between road and rail, or the differences made by changes in energy prices — would pave the way.

A POLICY FOR TRANSPORT

Alexander Grey*

In anticipation of the Government's long awaited public consultation paper on transport policy, which is reported to be coming out within the next week or so, I make no apology for opening this conference with a broad sketch of some of the things that I would have liked to see in this document. But first, I shall go back in history for a moment to set some of our current problems in context.

Historical background

Less than two hundred years ago most people in this country lived their whole lives without travelling beyond the boundaries of the village where they were born. But with the development of new forms of transport, people's opportunities to get further away from their birth places with greater ease, speed and safety were gradually extended.

The rapid growth in demand for travel associated with these new transport facilities gave rise to considerable social and environmental problems, particularly in cities. Thus when the horse and carriage began to be used to carry people who had previously walked, and to move heavy goods which had been carried mainly on water, this led to a tremendous growth in congestion, stench and accidents. Photographs of the Thames bridges clogged with traffic at the turn of the century give a good picture of what the situation must have been like.

These urban problems were considerably eased with the rapid changeover to electric trams and motorbuses during the first twenty years of this century, since with their greater speed and larger carrying capacity far fewer vehicles were needed to carry the same number of passengers. There then followed a golden age for public road transport leading to a zenith in 1950 when the number of passenger journeys reached its peak. But in urban areas the dilemma experienced previously with the horse and carriage began to occur all over again, this time with the car. As more and more people opted to buy and use cars in order to travel faster, more comfortably and reliably, there soon came a point at which the extra congestion and environmental pollution which was thereby created made everyone worse off, including those travelling by car.

* Assistant Chief Planner (Public Transport), Greater London Council. This paper expresses only the personal views of the author.

Although traffic congestion is not a problem in rural areas, the transport situation has become no less serious. Rising car ownership made it increasingly uneconomic to provide a bus service to isolated villages for the declining numbers of people who were still dependent on it, and the resulting reductions and withdrawals have created real hardship.

Do people need to travel?

Because of these problems many people are now wondering whether we are really better off as a result of wider opportunities to travel much further than our ancestors; and doubts of this kind are often associated with worries about the health of modern society and the danger of too rapid a growth in consumption and wealth. Ivan Illich has argued that motorised transport has enslaved the human race and imposed glaring social inequalities, and that we should return to societies and patterns of living based on 'self-powered mobility'.[1] Motorised transport would still be available for the sick, disabled, the lazy and others who needed it, but kept in a subordinate role by not being allowed to exceed a speed limit of about 25 mph at the very most.

'Free people must travel the road to productive social relations at the speed of a bicycle' is a typical quote from his treatise. But unfortunately that is not much help if there is no one you can stand who lives within cycling distance. More seriously, it would be unwise to deny the widening of horizons and interests that is made possible by the ability to travel quickly over long distances. Illich himself has been educated in no less than three different countries, and worked and travelled in several more, not always on a bicycle; and so he has already been able to envelop cultural and social diversity within his own personality. But most of us still depend on future opportunities to travel in order to widen our horizons, and indeed the extent to which we still rely on self-powered mobility is often not sufficiently appreciated. According to the National Travel Survey about two fifths of all journeys are still made on foot,[2] and of course there has been a rapid growth in cycling over the last year or so – as is signified by the photograph in *The Times* this morning of Baroness Birk riding rather unsteadily on a bicycle through Hyde Park, following the intensive practice sessions she is reported to have undertaken in the corridors of power at Marsham Street (or should I say corridors of powered mobility).

Transport for people

So transport policy makers would do well to take careful account of Illich's observations as a backcloth to whatever decisions they take on improving transport facilities. It is particularly important to ensure that their decisions are sharply focussed on people's transport needs, and only incidentally on passenger car units, modal splits, generalised costs, semi-linked journeys, and other pieces of technical apparatus. Strangely enough, this might have seemed a revolutionary heresy only two or three years ago; but thanks to the pioneering work of people like Mayer Hillman, to whom much of the credit must be due, there is now a fairly widespread consensus that social and humanitarian considerations should be at the forefront of decisions on transport policy in the public sector.

In pursuing these social aims, however, we must not allow ourselves to become submerged in what the chairman of my Transport Committee has described in a recent public document as a 'surfeit of visionary planning, often leaving only a trail of social conflict'.[3] Whether as transport researchers, planners, consumers, consultants, civil servants, local government officers or members of local government transport committees, I believe that our main attention should be devoted to improving the efficiency with which the various transport facilities are provided and operated, and the effectiveness with which people can reach their transport objectives or be supplied with the goods they need – all within the existing pattern of human settlements. But solutions to the transport problem must, of course, also relate to the broader context determined by whatever opportunities might be available for changing the location of homes, shops, offices, schools and other travel objectives.

An efficient transport policy

Although social aims must be the prime determinant of transport policy, it is in a way even more important to ensure that the actual transport systems for moving goods and people about are chosen, designed and managed as efficiently as possible. This in turn involves maximising the amount of travel that people can make within that social context, and in the light of the financial and environmental constraints that the community has decided to lay down. Even in Illich's economy, transport policy-makers would still have as their prime concern issues like whether a change from one man to two man operated cycle rickshaws would allow for sufficient improvements in speed and capacity to justify the increase in operating costs.

To appraise efficiency it is useful to have a clear, simple and unambiguous criterion for choosing between different programmes and projects. For public passenger transport, one of the most useful tools of that kind that has so far been developed is the criterion now employed by the GLC and London Transport, which ranks projects according to the number of extra passenger miles they generate per pound of net cost. Like all techniques this one has its limitations, principally that it is less suitable for choosing between projects that involve wide differences in journey distance and speed (such as improvements to local bus services versus Inter-City railway services, or walking and pedestrian facilities versus motorised movement). As with cost-benefit analysis, this technique is also concerned primarily with comparative efficiency and is not intended to cover wider social or strategic issues. But for motorised travel, in not too large a geographical area, it can be applied to a wide range of projects (from the building of new roads and railway lines to moving bus stops or changing frequencies on a particular bus route), and can shed new light on their comparative advantage. Off-peak service improvements on the Victoria Line, for example, appear to generate about 100 passenger miles per pound, compared with about 30 from the GLC's recent investment in the North London Line, 20 for certain bus service improvements, and only 1.5 for the proposed new underground line from Strand to Fenchurch Street (Fleet Line Stage 2) and then on along the river through Docklands to Thamesmead (the River Line). It is likely that even lower returns would be obtained from most new road investments, and the general implication of this kind of analysis is that the main emphasis of transport policy should be on getting the most out of existing assets and operations before major extensions to the transport system are contemplated. This is particularly so in a town like London which already has a comparatively dense network of roads and railway lines, and indeed the same conclusion was drawn in the major joint study by GLC, DoE, BR and LT of London's railway services which was completed at the end of 1974. But the Fleet/River Line can be justified by wider planning, development and environmental considerations, which should also be the test of any other major extensions to the rail or road networks.

With freight, an output-oriented criterion of this type does not seem necessary, since strict financial considerations can be the main test. The central aim of policy might be to ensure that raw materials and finished goods are transported between ports, factories, warehouses and shops, and then to their destinations, by whatever combination of air, road, rail and water transport means the lowest total cost in resources. Because of the severe environmental damage and resource costs imposed by heavy lorries, however, it seems clear that the government should use a combination of regulations, controls and fiscal policies to reduce their noise, vibration and pollution, to reinforce the more efficient use of vehicles by (for example) discouraging empty or part-loaded running, and finally to check the continual erosion in the competitive position of the railway. On this last point the government's actions might include the use of its powers under section 8 of the Railways Act 1974 to pay capital grants for the provision or improvement of private sidings, depots, container terminals and other facilities; and a postponement of the instruction to the Railways Board that rail freight should be self financing until such time as taxes on heavy goods vehicles had been raised to a level at which they bore a fairer share of the costs they imposed on the community. This might also avoid the danger of section 8 grants being given (say) for railway sidings, but with no trains actually running on them because BR were unable to offer competitive charges.

Of course, rail is not nearly as suitable as road for many, some would say most, types of load and distribution pattern, and in 1974 carried only just over a quarter as much in terms of ton mileage.[4] But only twenty years previously more freight had gone by rail than by road, and it should be possible to exert at least some restraining influence on this rapid decline in competitive position, particularly in relation to the goods carried over longer distances by heavy lorries in which there has been the most rapid growth. (There was, for example, nearly a 25 fold increase between 1954 and 1974 in the number of lorries of over eight tons unladen weight.)

Passenger transport in towns

Going back to the previous conclusion that urban transport decisions should aim to get the most out of existing assets, bus priority provides a good example of what can be done at present. The main trouble is that really attractive returns can only be obtained from bus priority schemes if they are implemented on a sufficient scale along particular bus routes to enable the same service frequencies to be maintained with less buses and crews. The GLC's proposed speedbus routes into central London, for example, appear to yield very high returns as a result of the extensive bus priority measures, with the savings obtained on the ordinary buses sufficient to enable the new speedbus services to be put on at no extra cost, and the gain in bus receipts offsetting the financial cost of implementation by a large margin. But with no countervailing traffic restraint measures, this could only be at the expense of much worse environmental conditions on certain residential roads resulting from car traffic diverted from the bus routes. Considerable concern has been expressed on this point during the public consultations that the GLC has been holding.

To avoid dilemmas of this kind, a more radical and total approach to passenger transport in towns seems necessary. The main aim would be to achieve a sharp reduction in the number of private cars that are at present clogging up our city centres, through a combination of strict physical controls over their use at peak periods and in congested places, and differential pricing and fiscal policies. Bearing in mind the enormous number of vehicles involved (for example about two thirds of the vehicles on the roads in central London are cars, compared with about a fifth for goods vehicles, and going right down to around two per cent for buses) it is likely that such a policy could improve the overall efficiency of the transport system in several ways: for example through

large savings in bus operating costs and/or higher service frequencies;
commercial benefits resulting from the much freer movement of delivery vans and lorries;
faster and more reliable travelling times for everyone on average, with large benefits for those previously travelling by public transport, and with little disadvantage (and for some even a slight improvement) for those previously travelling by car;

much greater mobility for those without access to a car;

lower fuel consumption;

a reduction in accidents, noise, fumes and visual intrusion.

Since the roads would be free from traffic congestion, it might well be possible to make bus services profitable in many British cities at current fare levels charged to passengers and wage levels paid to operating staff. But it would be by no means an easy task to ensure that urban public transport undertakings really took full advantage of the opportunities they were given to offer a really attractive alternative to the banned private car. For this would require all forms of rail and public road transport to be managed not only with efficiency, but also with imagination, flexibility and drive — characteristics which do not always come easily to large public sector corporations. The initiatives taken by the Tyne and Wear County Council and Passenger Transport Executive provide a good example of what might be done. There a new light railway system or 'Metro' is being designed as part of an integrated public transport system, coordinated in terms of routeing, timetabling, interchange, etc. with restructured short and long distance bus services. The intention is also to disentangle the Metro from the main British Rail organisation, so as to achieve benefits in flexibility, efficiency and cost saving.

More generally, the particular pieces of the public transport jigsaw should be designed and slotted together according to what capacity, journey distance and frequency was required at different places and times of day. To achieve high and reliable frequencies at low costs in terms of energy, manpower and environmental disruption, local authorities should also be willing to experiment with new forms of automated transport, taking account of the experiments now being conducted in the United States and other countries.

With public road transport, the need is more for institutional than for technological innovation. Flexible, decentralised systems of management and control are needed, above all to run the conventional bus services properly. Beyond that, they are also needed to coordinate the interests of private bus operators, the taxi trade, and other agencies, and to experiment with new forms of 'intermediate' transport such as dial-a-bus, jitneys, taxi sharing and car sharing.

British Rail's Passenger Services

The Newcastle method also suggests what could be the first of a three-pronged approach to the running and financing of BR's passenger services. This might involve disentangling the local and commuter passenger services in all conurbations (including London) from the rest of BR's mammoth operation, and having them run on behalf of the relevant local authorities as part of their integrated urban transport systems. Service, subsidy and fare levels for the local

14

railway services would thus be decided by local and not central government, in line with the procedures adopted in principle (if not yet carried out in practice) for all the metropolitan counties. Secondly, BR would manage all its Inter-City and the South Eastern outer suburban passenger services on a cost-covering basis on behalf of central government. Thirdly, all the non-profitable parts of BR's passenger network apart from local services in conurbations would be subsidised, as appropriate, by central government on social grounds, going back to the principles adopted in the Transport Act 1968 which the government unnecessarily departed from in the blanket deficit financing approach of the Railways Act 1974. In addition, there would of course need to be a vigorous attack on costs and productivity across the whole board, about which we will be hearing more from Richard Pryke, and to which the new chairman will no doubt be giving his closest attention. It would also be necessary for all three parties – central government, local government, and BR – to adopt a strict marginal approach to changes in costs and revenues, which recognises the high fixed cost nature of railway operation, and avoids the hopelessly uneconomic cuts in services that have been planned for this year.

Transport in rural areas

The government's direct subsidies to BR passenger services would thus be restricted mainly to railways serving the less densely populated parts of the country. There the private car is undoubtedly the most appropriate form of passenger transport since there is no problem of traffic congestion, and individual journey patterns and demand levels make it very difficult to provide even conventional bus services on an economic basis. Transport policy in rural areas could therefore have a different emphasis, aimed at encouraging rather than restricting car use. However, nearly a third of households in rural areas do not own a car, and there is an urgent need to provide for them a transport service that uses scarce resources more efficiently than is possible with the conventional bus and train services on their own.

Considerable opportunities for improving efficiency exist as a result of the almost total lack of coordination between the wide range of road transport services that connect isolated villages, and the local railway lines and stations. The road services include parcel deliveries by no less than four different public operators (two subsidiaries of the National Freight Corporation – National Carriers Ltd and Roadline UK, together with British Rail's Express Parcels Service, and the Post Office); delivery vans for milk, bread, meat and groceries; school buses; and of course the ordinary bus services where they still exist. To coordinate such diverse activities with each other and with the railways requires an imaginative approach to social action in the public sector, which might also depend upon unusual institutional innovations.

The Postbus service is a good start in this direction. The hundredth Postbus was recently opened to connect 14 isolated villages in Wigtownshire, Scotland. As well as carrying mail and passengers, it delivers groceries, milk and even doctors' prescriptions. But a positive and creative lead by the government on a much broader front could yield higher dividends and help the public sector to win back some of the respect it has lost in recent years.

This solution, with the car supplemented by special forms of intermediate transport and ordinary public transport playing a relatively minor role, should be thought of as a model for areas with really low population densities. In contrast, the model policy for high density urban areas would put these three types of transport service in precisely the reverse order, with ordinary buses and trains playing the dominant role, and very substantial reductions in the numbers of private cars on the road. In practice, however, there will be many situations in which local authorities will find it appropriate to implement a policy somewhere in between these two extremes: in outer suburban areas, and in city centres outside peak periods, for example.

Regulation and control

It would be much easier to encourage the development of flexible public and intermediate transport systems in cities if there were a considerable relaxation in the regulations and controls that now exist over buses, taxis and car sharing. This could also provide an attractive offset to the much tougher controls over lorries and private cars that would have been introduced as part of the plan to encourage a shift back to public transport. Few people would wish to go back to the anarchic, cut-throat situation found in the 1920s, when an enterprising free-lance operator could put on a new bus service whenever and wherever he liked, provided he had obtained a licence for the vehicle. But the situation may now have swung too far to the opposite extreme, and a careful study into the possibilities of relaxing the present controls over bus and taxi operations is needed.

In rural areas, relaxation of controls is also necessary as part of the positive approach to the coordination of goods and passenger services that I have just mentioned. This would need to go much further than the relaxations in the public service vehicle licencing code which the government intend to introduce on an experimental basis in three or four rural counties,[5] and cover (for example) car insurance, EEC regulations, and the rules governing the operation of parcels and small goods delivery.

An effective transport policy

A transport system designed in this way, to enhance the efficiency with which people and goods are moved from one place to another, ought to make things better for everyone on average. But with passenger transport we must also be concerned with how effectively the system caters for the special needs of individuals. The main aims here might be to ensure a certain minimum level of transport availability for people who would otherwise tend to be left out (the poor, the old, the young, the disabled, etc.); and to prevent a regressive redistribution of income from poor to rich people.

Minimum standards

The approach to minimum standards would involve local authorities in taking initiatives of various kinds, such as:

> concessionary fare schemes, like the free bus travel for old people outside peak hours that is available in London;

> measures to protect pedestrians and cyclists from danger and inconvenience;

> modifications to vehicles, station access, and other parts of the transport system, so as to make it easier for elderly and disabled people to use them (lower step heights on buses, for example).

There should be no problem in taking such initiatives as part of the transport strategy described earlier, though the government might need to specify certain minimum standards for local councils and transport operators to follow. Special earmarked grants might be made available to ensure that the standards laid down were achieved. Central government would also need to make sure that this approach was coordinated between the DoE and other relevant government departments, so that consistent standards of accessibility to hospitals, schools, child welfare clinics and so on were specified and adhered to.

Income distribution

The transport strategy recommended for rural areas, with more efficient forms of 'intermediate' public transport being actively developed to supplement the private car which would continue to be the main mode of passenger travel, can only have a favourable effect on income distribution. In towns the situation is a little more complicated, since the strategy depends upon introducing an appropriate combination of higher taxes and tougher controls on private motoring, and comparatively lower public transport fare levels. The effects of such a policy on income distribution would depend first upon whether the changes in relative prices cancelled each other out: that is, on whether any net reduction in income from public transport fares (resulting from the lower fare levels, offset to some extent by the higher demand) were matched by the increased revenue from the higher charges imposed on private motorists. If this were the case, the policy change would be progressive, since richer people tend to own and use private cars much more than poorer. On the other hand if the policy led to an increase in the amount of subsidy for the transport system as a whole, the effects on income distribution would depend on what sort of tax increases were made to pay for the extra subsidy.

A fair amount of misunderstanding has arisen on this point because of a lack of appreciation that the impact on income distribution depends on the chosen tax/subsidy combination, not just on the subsidy itself. Thus it has been shown that although higher rates are regressive in their impact, higher bus fares are even more so; from which it can be concluded that subsidies for bus travel could be progressive even if financed entirely out of the rates.[6] This would not be so for rail travel in general, but joint subsidies to bus and inner suburban rail services in conurbations are also likely to be progressive if financed by the right combination of central and local government grant. This is particularly true in Tyne and Wear, where the Metro has been designed to serve high unemployment and low income areas. The most regressive form of subsidy would be to BR's Inter-City services, but even here the policy might be progressive if financed out of income tax.

Control of subsidies

Any subsidy paid by government bodies to public transport operators does, of course, need to be closely monitored and controlled in relation to carefully defined objectives. It hardly needs saying (unless there is anyone here from the *Daily Express* or the Department of the Environment) that it is perfectly feasible to achieve this without eroding management efficiency or incentives to improved performance. The practice currently followed by the GLC and London Transport provides a good example of what can be done. And a comparison between, for example, subsidy and efficiency levels in British and continental national railway undertakings shows that there is not an automatic correlation between high subsidy and high inefficiency.

Another point which does not appear to be sufficiently appreciated by many civil servants is that fares subsidies should be treated as transfer payments from the taxpayer's to the passenger's pocket. Curtailment of such subsidies is irrelevant to the government's attempts at controlling inflation and easing the pressure on real resources. What needs to be done is to ensure that scarce real resources are used to the best effect; and indeed one of the main reasons for recommending a return to the situation in which most travel in town centres takes place by public transport, is that far less real resources (in terms of fuel, vehicles, staff, road maintenance, etc.) would be needed to cater for the same amount of travel.

The real reason for restraining the growth in revenue subsidies must surely be because of a feeling that the higher tax levels cannot be tolerated politically, and that view has in fact been clearly expressed by Mr Crosland in a recent *Guardian* article.[7] Let us hope that he has passed the message on to his civil servants, and that the forthcoming Consultation Document will not continue to disguise the real issue.

Widening of horizons

However, even though higher subsidy levels need not lead to a regressive redistribution of income from poor to rich people, they would create a greater demand for and hence require more resources to be devoted to transport. Whether this is a good thing or not brings us back to the point I made at the beginning, about the widening of horizons that is made possible by the provision of greater opportunities for travel; though with a given amount of public expenditure in total, this can only be done at the expense of investment in other public services. What is really needed is a rational approach to resource allocation and a combined and consistent attack across the whole field, so that more varied travel opportunities are associated with a wider range of job opportunities, and of educational, cultural and recreational facilities.

The problems to be overcome in developing such an approach can be illustrated by reference to one of the social groups that are currently 'disadvantaged' from the travel point of view, namely children. On average, children of school age appear to spend well over twenty hours a week watching television, so there is little point making it easier for them to travel in the evenings or at the weekends unless they are also given recreational facilities outside the home that are at least as attractive as what is currently their favourite pastime. And such a view is borne out by the fact that children in the lower income groups, who have less opportunity to indulge in other recreational pursuits, spend more than the average amount of time watching television.

A final important point to be borne in mind here is that if the gloomy forecasts of many commentators about the health of the British economy over the next ten years are anywhere near to being right, this might require a reduction (rather than a maintenance or increase) in the amount of travel. If this were so the improved quality of public services across the board which would result from the more flexible and imaginative approach to their provision could be an invaluable offset to the lower real incomes that people would have to suffer.

 Conclusions

The transport strategy I have suggested is intended not as a set of concrete proposals for action, but as a tentative description of the principles which might be followed in working out such proposals. These principles can be summarised as follows:

1. The main emphasis of transport policy should be on getting the most out of existing assets, operations and opportunities. Major new extensions to the road or railway networks would normally be justified only by wider land-use planning or environmental criteria, and should in any case not be considered seriously before possibilities in the former area had been exhaustively examined.

2. With freight policy, the government might use a combination of regulations, controls and fiscal policies to reduce the environmental damage caused by heavy lorries, and to restrain the continual erosion in the competitive position of rail in relation to road freight haulage.

3. For passenger transport in congested city centres, appropriate controls over private cars together with suitable taxing and pricing policies could be used to free roads from traffic congestion and make public transport and goods vehicles the main means of motorised transport in peak periods. The various public transport modes should be closely coordinated with each other. The whole system would need to be managed in a flexible, responsive and imaginative manner, particularly with regard to the management of the conventional bus and train services, but also taking account of opportunities that present themselves with regard to new technology and 'intermediate' forms of transport.

4. Private cars might be encouraged rather than restricted in rural areas. To cater for the substantial number of people who do not have access to a car, the various passenger, parcel and small goods delivery services which operate between villages could be coordinated with each other and the local bus and rail services. The Postbus is a start in the right direction, but initiatives on a broader front are needed.

5. Passenger transport policy outside peak periods and in areas of medium population density could be designed with a more even balance between conventional public transport, intermediate transport, and the private car.

6. Associated with whatever actions are taken to improve BR's costs and productivity across the board, the railway passenger services could be split into three distinct parts: local suburban and commuter services in all conurbations, including London, for which the policy and financial control would rest with local government; Inter-City and outer suburban services, which would be managed on behalf of central government on a cost-covering basis, but with a strict marginal approach to changes in costs and revenues; and other passenger services which would be subsidised as appropriate by central government on social grounds.

7. As a counterpart to the tougher controls over private motoring in towns, the possibility of relaxing existing controls over bus and taxi operation and car sharing could be considered. This would help encourage a more vigorous and competitive approach to the provision of public transport services, and narrow the tremendous gap between the quality of service offered by the car and the conventional bus. In rural areas, relaxation of controls would also make it easier to coordinate goods and passenger services along the lines suggested.

8. As part of this overall transport strategy special initiatives could be taken by

local authorities to ensure that minimum standards of transport accessibility were available for 'disadvantaged' groups of people. Central government might define minimum standards where appropriate, and consider paying special earmarked grants to ensure that these standards were attained.

9. The wider opportunities made available as a result of improving the transport system must be associated with corresponding improvements in other public services, as part of a consistent approach to planning and resource allocation across the whole field.

Others here will no doubt attach higher priority to different principles from these, as I am sure we will be hearing during the conference. Above all, I hope that our exchange of ideas will put us all in a better position to work out a set of transport policies which are consistent with each other, with the objectives that have been set for them, and with the empirical evidence on which they are based.

Finally, on what is I think the hundredth anniversary of the invention in Germany of the first four-stroke cycle engine operating on the principle of the modern car engine, I would like to congratulate the Nuffield Foundation for organising this conference. Even though many of the things that will be said will undoubtedly be anti the private car in its present role, I am sure that Lord Nuffield, who started work by setting up a bicycle repair shop, would have been one of the first to recognise the need to find new ways of solving the acute transport problems we are currently faced with — after all that is precisely what he was doing with motor cars at the beginning of this century.

1. Ivan D. Illich, *Energy and Equity,* Calder and Boyars, 1974.
2. E. Daor and P. B. Goodwin, Variations in the importance of walking as a mode of travel. *GLTS Note* 205, GLC, November 1975.
3. *Transport — A Programme for Action 1976-77,* GLC, December 1975.
4. *Annual Abstract of Statistics 1975,* Table 252.
5. *Hansard,* 3 December 1975, Written Answers Cols. 613-4.
6. A. Grey, *Urban Fares Policy,* Saxon House, 1975.
7. A. Crosland, The Battle for the Public Purse, *Guardian,* 24 March 1976.

THE INTERACTION OF LIFE STYLES WITH RESIDENTIAL LOCATION AND ASSOCIATED PATTERNS OF TRAVEL

Mayer Hillman and Anne Whalley*

Public policies are concerned with the determination and promotion of measures identified as being in the public interest. Their common purpose is the improvement of the quality of life – the extension of the freedom of the individual and the maximisation of his choice so that he has ample opportunity of achieving his potential. However, it is commonly agreed that such improvement should only be made where the result can be seen not to be at the expense of disadvantaged members of society.

Hence there is a particular need for public policies to take a broad perspective of the wider consequences of individuals extending their own particular freedoms: it must not be presumed that what is desirable for small numbers of people in the fortunate position of being able to exercise wide choice is necessarily an appropriate or attainable aspiration for large numbers. This poses a very real dilemma for policy makers, particularly as there has been an enviable tradition within this country of minimising trespass on individual freedom.

It is necessary to make these preliminary remarks as we believe that transport policy should have a strong social content – as have most other areas of public policy – not least because of the social consequences stemming from its implementation. Indeed it may be the absence of an adequate social input into current policy that explains many of the problems which are the subject of this conference.

The tools that have been used to evaluate the appropriateness of past practices have reflected a continuing attempt to match the rising demand for motorised mobility by increasing the capacity of the transport network through road building and by management measures to improve traffic flow – a total process tempered by economic appraisal and by a concern to lessen the intrusiveness of the environmental damage, if necessary by financial compensation. Most effort has been directed towards reducing the costs of motorised travel to the individual.

This approach has been largely deficient in one significant respect – it does not adequately achieve the aim of maximising welfare and minimising need. This

* Research workers at Political and Economic Planning

deficiency can be seen in the toleration of the continuing horrific level of road accidents, which includes a thousand child deaths a year, in spite of the primary causes and cures being so well known. Further evidence lies in the fact that transport policy has focussed so much on the demands of the more mobile — those with access to a car — and of those forecast to be future beneficiaries of its undoubted attractions, rather than on the more basic needs of those without a car.

Indeed it is very surprising that social research has been carried out extensively into the consequences of planning policy, to the extent that there is much attention paid to anomie in high rise flats, the breakdown of communities in comprehensive redevelopment, to inner city vandalism and suburban blues; but very little consideration has been given to the social costs of personal travel or to the changes in personal behaviour and life style associated with different private and public decisions on transport. Yet an understanding of these is an essential prerequisite for formulating appropriate policies which have the minimum of adverse social consequences.

In formulating such transport policies, we must have knowledge of life styles, of their determinants and correlates, of interactions between people, and of the social implications of various types or aspects of life style, for these are undoubtedly associated with personal travel patterns.

At various times in life, changes occur in the areal component of personal travel — access to people and places — due to changes in location. They also occur in the personal component and are associated with changes in role or interest. In order to understand what adaptive processes need to be made when change occurs it is necessary to look at the characteristics of individuals and households in the different states and to examine the travel patterns that go with them. Then, to assess the desirability of the different states, the social implications affecting those involved in the changes must be understood.

Our research at PEP has given some indication of the wide variations in travel patterns among people in different situations — both personal and areal — and some of the findings of our studies are therefore relevant to discussion of the influence and impact of these changes.

The tables which follow show some of the complex relationships of accessibility, mobility and travel. The data have been extracted from surveys for studies conducted at PEP over the last few years: one set of self-completion surveys was carried out among adults, teenagers and children in five areas ranging from a rural parish, through different sized towns, to a ward in inner London (Five Areas' Survey). Another set of surveys was carried out in the South East's Outer Metropolitan Area: one of these was a large scale (15,000 households) postal survey (OMA Postal Survey), and the other two were personal interview surveys of pensioners and of young mothers (OMA Interview Surveys).

First, Table 1 gives a simple example of the effect of areas of residence on mobility and accessibility. Respondents living in rural areas are twice as likely as those in urban areas to have no Sunday bus service, though somewhat compensating for this are the higher levels of multiple car ownership in the rural areas. The compensation is partial because, as we shall see, the extent to which cars are available to different people within a household varies widely. In the lower part of the table, the poorer rural bus services are reflected in the lower level of bus use: the difference may appear small but is made more significant by the fact that motorised travel is often more necessary in rural areas, where fewer people have easy access on foot to facilities such as shops.

Table 1

	people living in:	
	urban areas	rural areas
	%	%
no Sunday bus	11	21
households without car	30	23
households with 2+ cars	16	23
bus use 1+ per week (adults)	42	34
shops within 5 mins. walk	67	53

Source: OMA Postal Survey

Our next table indicates the influence of another aspect of area of residence — distance to a town centre. Table 2 shows that the further people live from a town centre, the less likely it is that they will have commonly used facilities close at hand. People living very near the centre can, of course, use the centre itself, but the table illustrates the fact that those living further out are not compensated by having local sub-centres. Part of the explanation for the decline in local accessibility results from the lower densities of much private newer housing built on the outskirts of existing towns and, moreover, without the active participation of planners which occurred in the New Towns. Rather paradoxically the table also shows how people with easy access to a bus service are the ones most likely to have easy access on foot to the other facilities: they are getting the best of both worlds.

The influence of density, which can partly be construed from Table 2, can also be seen in the data in Table 3. Respondents were asked which out of nine commonly used facilities are within a ten minute walk of their homes. The results show the association of high density with good local accessibility. (It is worth noting here that the 'high' density in our surveys is nowhere near as high

Table 2

		within 5 minutes' walk		
if living at distance to town centre of:	shops %	post-office %	play-ground %	none of these %
up to ½m (under 10 mins walk)	87	70	47	8
1-1½m (20-29 mins walk)	65	50	42	24
2-4m (10-19 mins car)	58	47	38	30
over 4m (30 mins+ bus)	49	41	34	38
if has bus stop:				
within 5 mins walk	72	60	45	18
beyond 5 mins walk	45	34	29	40

Source: OMA Postal Survey

Table 3

		density		
of 9 facilities in common use:	rural %	low %	medium %	high %
at least 4 nearby	52	58	66	82
none nearby	14	9	8	1
bus service:				
stop within 5 mins	66	78	81	88
5-10 min service	0	0	29	12
15-20 min service	9	30	42	67
less than hourly	24	4	1	0

Source: OMA Interview Surveys

as inner city densities, but more like those of New Towns or indeed of the older parts of existing towns.) This table also relates density to the bus service, and again it can be seen that better services prevail in the higher density areas: they are more frequent and also more reliable.

Having shown that density is related both to bus service and to accessibility, **we can** now look at the effect on bus use. Table 4 shows greater use of buses

Table 4

young mothers' use of buses:	area character			density			
	large town	medium town	rural	high	medium	low	rural
	%	%	%	%	%	%	%
1+ per week	50	26	17	51	37	22	19
never	16	44	50	21	33	48	55
reason for low bus use:							
can walk	21	13	2	27	18	5	2
car available	30	53	60	35	37	60	68

Source: OMA Interview Surveys

in higher density areas and in towns, particularly large ones; in other words there is more use of buses where there is a better bus service. Though bus use does vary by area, its use is generally rather low. In low density and rural areas the car is more widely available and used, as we would expect; but in high density areas buses and cars are not the only competitors, as the table clearly shows, for many respondents mentioned walking as their main reason for not using buses. It is pertinent at this point to note that this survey was confined to young adults – children or elderly people could be expected to mention walking even more, for they have least access to cars.

One other point needs making in the light of this table. An earlier speaker made reference to the possibility of increasing mobility by improving public transport: such an aim is worthwhile, but it does need setting against the convenience of using buses. This convenience may not be very great, for the table shows that even in the area of good bus services only half the respondents use buses as often as once a week – not very high bus use bearing in mind the fact that trips by all methods of travel usually amount to eleven or twelve a week.

The tables so far have concentrated on areal variations, but it can be shown that people too vary in their level of personal mobility, and this plays an important role in shaping their day-to-day travel patterns.

Table 5 is one for women's lib! The table shows that, in car-owning households, the men are more than three times as likely as the women to have a driving licence, and he who holds a licence has far more influence on the use of the car. Men are also less likely to be in a household without a car and even in

26

these households it is quite probable that they can drive (though the table does not show this).

Table 5

	men %	women %
car availability:		
licence and household car	59	18
no licence but household car	5	35
no car in household	36	4

Source: Five Areas' Survey

Table 6

	density		
	low %	medium %	high %
young women with:			
'high' access to shops	21	62	80
optional car use	43	21	7
'day-to-day' shopping:			
walk	49	66	75
car	49	24	14
bus	3	10	11
area used by young women:			
local shops	40	61	65
town centre	60	39	36
young women shop frequently	40	50	66

Source: OMA Interview Surveys

Age, as well as sex, helps determine mobility, not surprisingly as the car has become 'widely available' only during the last twenty years. Elderly people are not often found in car-owning households, and elderly women have particularly low car availability as many of them live alone and rely solely on their state pension.

Variations in mobility have consequences for travel patterns; the surveys showed that although the weekly total of trips for men and women are remarkably similar, women on the whole make not far short of twice as many walk trips. A further influence on travel is the location of people's homes, due to the association with access noted earlier. If we take shopping as an example (for it is a frequent activity, shoppers averaging about four trips a week), the joint influences of mobility and access can be detected, as in Table 6. This table shows first, the change in balance for low and high density areas between on the one hand low access to shops but high access to cars and, on the other hand, high access to shops but low access to cars; second, an equivalent variation in the methods of travel used for shopping, with very low bus use overall; and third, a variation in the shopping trips made, both in terms of the type of area used and the frequency of the trip. In short the women in high density areas with shops nearby are likely to use their local shops, to use them frequently, and to go on foot; the women in low density areas have greater access to cars than to shops and so more of them drive when shopping, go to town centres and go shopping less often.

Turning to another survey group, pensioners, it is clear that, as Table 7 shows, age takes its toll both physically (almost a third having some physical disability which hinders walking) and financially (almost two thirds have no household car). Physical disability also in fact hinders their use of buses, with high bus platforms causing a particular problem, so that the more disabled respondents in our survey are the ones less likely to use buses. Neither are they more likely to live in a car-owning household: indeed a relatively high proportion live carless and alone.

Moreover, a higher than average proportion are without a telephone of their own. Yet these are the people who in theory could benefit most from our motorised, technologically oriented society.

Table 7

pensioners' mobility

physical disability 31%	no household car 62%	household car but no licence 22%	household car and licence 15%	no 'phone 51%

pensioners' method of travel

	social visits	clubs	library	church	cinema etc.	open space	day-to-day shopping
walk	56	45	50	62	29	53	64
bus	15	17	20	4	24	21	19
car	29	38	30	35	48	26	17

Source: OMA Interview Surveys

The second half of the table shows the predominance of walking for pensioners' day-to-day activities. This is a consequence of their relatively low car ownership and the commonly cited difficulties of using buses. Clearly the fact that two thirds of them can make use of concessionary bus fares does not enhance the attractiveness of this method of travel to any great extent.

At the other end of the age spectrum is another group with particular mobility or travel problems, though these result more from parental restrictions than from difficulty in getting about on foot. Children can walk, unaided, from the age of 12 to 15 months, but Table 8 shows that in the OMA survey all the children attending pre-school facilities, three quarters of those at infant school and over a quarter at junior school are taken to and collected from school each day – and this in spite of the short distances involved. The main reason given by their mothers is traffic danger. This answer clearly relates to the type of journey involved as the table illustrates: perhaps it should be pointed out that even with no road to cross, the child may have to walk along a heavily trafficked highway.

Table 8

route to school involves crossing

	main road no patrol %	main road with patrol %	side road %	no road %
percentage of primary school children* accompanied	65	48	41	27

* infants and juniors

Source: OMA Interview Surveys

	age of child			
	7	8	9	10
% not allowed to cross main road alone	54	35	30	5
% not allowed to use buses alone	84	68	47	21

Source: Five Areas' Survey

The survey of Five Areas confirms the restrictions on children: a third of them are not allowed to cross roads alone, the restriction being more widespread among the youngest ones (aged 7) and less among the oldest (aged 11). Buses, which generally are routed along major roads with heavy traffic on them, are 'out of bounds' for half the children. Moreover, virtually all children are able to ride a cycle and two thirds in the survey own one; but only one per cent of these junior school children cycle to school — a proportion far removed from the equivalent one for their car-owning fathers driving to work. In relation to cycling, over half the mothers in the OMA survey gave 10 as the age at which they would allow their children to cycle on main roads.

Areal variations in traffic danger can be seen from the children's survey too; one of the survey areas was in inner London, and there the restrictions are more extensively applied. This seems very unfair for these children are also the ones with the least compensating benefit of parents taking them about by car, as car ownership is lowest in the inner London area.

The table indicates how restrictions are lifted as the children grow older: a comparison can also be made between them and teenagers, who were also surveyed in the Five Areas. We found that less than half the outside activities of the younger group are undertaken alone or with friends (and this includes 'just playing around outside'), whereas for the teenagers the proportion is two thirds.

Our last table relates to teenagers, most of whom of course cannot drive. Car use therefore comes in third place for their day-to-day travel, with both car and bus falling far short of walking, except for the journeys to work of those over 15. The wish to be independent of parents is strong amongst teenagers, the surveys indicating this by showing how little they travel with parents. Even when they do travel by car, half the teenagers' trips are made in cars which do not belong to their own household. Finally, the table shows how rarely cycles are used as a travel method, even among this group for whom they could be particularly useful: it must be assumed that the danger and unpleasantness of cycling in heavy traffic is in large part to blame for this unreleased potential.

Table 9

teenagers' trips:		travel method				
		walk	bus	car	cycle	other
leisure/social/shop	%	46	20	22	9	3
school	%	47	30	6	11	2
work	%	16	49	29	6	8

Source: Five Areas' Survey

It is clear that travel patterns are a function of mobility and accessibility; they also result from the roles that people play in their lives. What remains to be discussed are the social implications that can be drawn out of the data, for these need consideration in formulating a policy for transport.

A few pertinent examples can be cited. First, there is a social — almost moral — issue relating to people's **freedom** to get around independently, if they wish to, and to travel where they choose. We have all heard tell of the freedom-giving potential of the car, but this needs to be set against the restriction of freedom of other road users which largely stems from car use: the circumscription of children's lives − not being allowed to cross roads or to cycle − represents a significant loss. Concomitantly, the need that parents feel to accompany their children to school represents a major imposition in terms of the time taken on the double journeys that parents make for each one made by the child. And in both instances there are side effects which are partly attributable to these restrictions. These effects may or may not be desirable: children watching television for an average of 24 hours a week, for instance, and mothers' lives necessarily being more child-centred than they would otherwise be.

In the case of teenagers, a rising proportion of whom have to go to school by special bus, there is less opportunity to take part in extra-curricular activities because of the difficulties of getting home. And this age group in particular suffers from the poorer off-peak bus services upon which they depend for many of their preferred leisure activities in the company of peers rather than that of their parents.

Secondly, there is the issue of **fear**. People have an understandable concern about traffic danger − many pensioners experience anxiety in getting off pavements and crossing roads; some people do not get licences because of a fear of driving (in our survey of young mothers one in five non-licence holders in car-owning households gave this reason); some fear molestation when using footpaths because of reduced pedestrian activity along them, and particularly in the specially provided 'safe' routes through underpasses; but most of all, as noted earlier, the fear of able bodied parents is reflected in their taking their able bodied children to and from school and other destinations for the safety of the children.

Thirdly, there is the issue of **inequity** − the existence of very unequal levels of mobility providing for some wide and for others narrow choice. Consider these anomalies:

1. Public transport service is likely to be at its lowest in areas where it is most needed − the low density areas tend to have the highest levels of car ownership *and* the fewest facilities accessible on foot.

2. Pensioners who have difficulty getting around on foot are also among the groups least likely to have access to a car.

3. People living in inner urban areas generally travel less than those in suburban or rural areas, yet the former are far more exposed to the nuisance from the latters' travel patterns than vice versa.

4. Increases in the scale of provision of shops, schools and hospitals are associated with longer journeys which are thereby less able to be made on foot; this is especially disadvantageous to people without the optional use of a car − but these are the people who are most likely to visit such facilities.

Finally, there is the social consequence of rising **private and public expenditure** as car ownership levels rise. Support for public transport in a declining market makes increasing inroads into limited public funds. This situation is made more extreme by urban forms matched to the needs of cars, because this results in low density housing and dispersed activities both of which are unsuited to public transport operations. Yet paradoxically in central urban areas there are also extra costs attendant upon maintaining the excessively 'peaked' services that stem from the necessary traffic restraint policies introduced at these times to reduce congestion. This contradictory situation has its origins in past incentives and planning policies which have encouraged people to live far from their place of work. There is also increasing personal expenditure on transport stemming from incentives to adopt a car-oriented way of life: this is particularly so in newer areas of low density housing where most adults have to aspire to optional car use and where it is difficult to provide 'everyday' facilities within easy walking distance.

There is not time now to go into more detail on these aspects of social concern or to do more than mention the other obvious area of concern — the quality of the environment. However, it may be appropriate at this stage to spell out the need for research oriented towards understanding the interaction of people's day-to-day patterns within the household and the more pervasive decisions of adults on such matters as car ownership and home location: changes in these affect the individual, the family and the wider community.

The complex trade-offs, the motivations, the adaptive processes, the deterrents and the satisfactions associated with these changes comprise an ill-researched area. Here are just a few examples:

Father takes a new job with longer journeys to work, thereby affecting:

a) the free time he has to spend with his family
b) the extent of his dependency on motorised transport
c) the travel patterns of the members of his family
d) the family budget
e) the future choice of home location.

The family decision to move home results in:

a) uprooting social ties
b) changed allocation of household budget for transport purposes
c) varying the access of all members of the house to their destinations
d) varying the need to accompany young children on their journeys.

The transfer of children from primary to secondary school is likely to entail:

a) longer journeys with higher travel costs and inconvenience

b) problems of travel due to the wish to take part in extra-curricular activities
c) altered friendship patterns and a need for greater mobility.

The acquisition or loss of a car:

a) affects the household budget with repercussions on other items of preferred expenditure
b) creates an incentive to maximise its use when acquired and a need for substitution systems when lost
c) changes social and leisure patterns due to the change in personal mobility.

The aftermath of a road accident resulting in serious injury may:

a) require becoming reconciled to disfigurement or disability
b) cause social changes owing to a change in economic circumstances
c) require coming to terms with the fact that it could have been avoided
d) result in a change of attitude towards motor travel.

Policy decisions in transport and related fields clearly should not be made in isolation from an appreciation of their possible social effects, for some will induce desirable and some undesirable outcomes whilst others will have mixed consequences. For example, a sharp increase in the price of petrol is likely to encourage lower driving speeds which in turn will reduce the number and severity of road accidents and may make it safer to cross roads on foot and to cycle on them; on the other hand, the extent of discretionary travel by motorised means would probably be curtailed, essential trips take longer, the cost of goods in the shops rise marginally and the revenue derived by the state from the tax on petrol be reduced because of lower sales. Likewise, the tightening of the law on company car ownership would oblige beneficiaries to match their leisure use of cars more closely to their real costs; this would thereby reduce the amount of car traffic, lower the rate of growth in car ownership, and encourage the import of foreign cars which tend to be more economical in their use of fuel, thus having adverse consequences for the British motor industry.

However it is not just decisions on travel within the family or the implementation of transport policy measures which have ramifications far wider than those intended. The Department of Health and Social Security has to treat in its hospitals over a third of a million people each year for their injuries in road accidents, largely as a consequence of the interaction of high speed limits and human fallibility. The use of motor vehicles for travel which is not entirely essential has adversely affected the Exchequer's balance of payments in view of the need to purchase oil from overseas; likewise inessential travel runs counter to the energy-saving policy of the Department of Energy. This policy is also rendered less effective by some of the policies of the Department of the Environment and of local authorities which encourage the development of low density housing or permit the construction of out-of-town shopping centres. Clearly there is a need for these different agencies to work corporately towards objectives commonly agreed to be in the public's wider interests.

If a more humane society is to be created in which we can all flourish as individuals then policies need to be formulated with a wider understanding of the direct and indirect changes that they induce. It is not only observed patterns of travel which should be used for determining appropriate policies, but also an evaluation of that travel and of other behavioural consequences of present policies. We must know far more of the social costs and benefits so that both public policies and personal decisions can be modified for the wider benefit of the community.

MISCONCEPTIONS ON MOBILITY

Richard Pryke*

Before considering the specific arguments for and against subsidising public transport, it is desirable to take a look at the extent to which mobility has increased and to discover whether the benefits have been confined to a relatively narrow section of the community. The belief that they have is one of the underlying assumptions of those who consider that public transport should be assisted on a large scale.

The increase in the quantity and quality of travel

The postwar period has seen an enormous and almost uninterrupted increase in the aggregate distance that individuals travel by public and private transport. In 1938, as the Table shows, the total passenger mileage in Great Britain was around 100 billion, including cycles but excluding walking. In 1958 the figure exceeded 150 billion for the first time. By 1964 the passenger mileage had risen to 200 billion and in 1970 it reached 250 billion. By 1973 the figure was up to 283 billion, although there was a slight reduction in 1974 as a result of the energy crisis and the large increase in the price of petrol.

Not only has there been a large rise in the quantity of travel but there has also been a marked improvement in its quality. Even the car's most severe critics concede that it is, for most types of journey, swifter and more convenient than public transport. 'The superiority of the car over the bus in terms of total travel time is well established,' writes Dr Mayer Hillman: 'surveys in different areas in Britain have shown door-to-door times by bus are two and four times as long as by car, over distances of one and three to five miles respectively.'[1]Although rail is both fast and convenient for longer journeys it too is much slower than car where distances are relatively short, and the bicycle must be regarded as an inferior mode of transport.[2] Cycling has steadily declined and was declining well before the growth of motor traffic can have had a seriously discouraging effect. In 1938 cars and motorcycles only accounted for a third of total passenger mileage and the bus and the bicycle had a combined share of almost 45 per cent. However, by the late 1950s the car was responsible for half of all passenger

* Senior Lecturer, Department of Economics, University of Liverpool

mileage, and by 1973 for nearly 80 per cent. Meanwhile buses and cycles accounted for as little as 13 per cent.

Total passenger transport in Great Britain
(billion passenger miles)

	Air	Rail	Bus and Coach etc.	Cars Taxis and Motorcycles		Cycles	Total
1938	–	23.3	28.0	33.0*	..	17.1	101.4
1952	0.1	24.1	50.1	37.9	(15.2)	14.2	126.4
1953	0.2	24.1	50.7	42.1	(17.2)	12.9	130.0
1958	0.3	25.5	43.4	72.9	(33.3)	8.8	150.9
1964	0.9	23.0	40.3	132.1	(61.7)	5.0	201.3
1970	1.2	22.2	34.8	189.9	(87.2)	2.6	250.7
1973	1.5	21.9	33.8	223.5	(100.3)	2.2	282.9
1974	1.4	22.4	33.6	217.5	(97.6)	2.1	277.0

* An occupancy rate of 1.8 per car and taxi mile was assumed.
(Note the figures in brackets show the number of passenger miles by private motor transport less the number of vehicle miles by car, taxi and motorcycle.)

Source: Richard Stone and D. A. Row, *The Measurement of Consumers' Expenditure and Behaviour in the United Kingdom* 1920-1938. Cambridge University Press, 1966, Vol. 2, pp. 64, 67, 71; J. R. Scott and J. C. Tanner, Traffic Trends and Vehicle-miles in Great Britain, 1938-1960, *The Surveyor,* 12 May 1962, p. 645; Department of the Environment, *Passenger Transport in Great Britain 1972,* HMSO, 1973, Table 1; *1973,* HMSO, 1975, Table 1; *Transport Statistics, Great Britain 1964-1974,* HMSO, 1976, Tables 9, 22.

It is widely believed that, as a result of congestion caused by the increase in car traffic, the car has become a slower and less convenient mode and that public transport has deteriorated in standard. If only because of the marked improvement in the quality of the service that BR provides, it seems very doubtful whether there has, on balance, been any decline in the quality of public transport. During the postwar period there has been a dramatic rise in the speed of Inter-City trains and some increase in their convenience due to the progressive adoption of even-interval time-tables.[3] There has also been some improvement in BR's other services as a result of the replacement of steam by diesel and electric traction. Little information is available about road speeds but what there is suggests that since the war speeds have remained about the same in towns and have increased on inter-city roads.[4]

Measurements at four sites on main roads near London, carried out at various dates between 1947 and 1955, showed that car speeds had increased by about one mph per annum.[5] A somewhat more extensive set of recordings in 1957 and 1964 at 15 sites on rural main roads within 70 miles of London also indicated that speeds were rising by around one mph a year.[6] There was not necessarily a corresponding increase in journey speeds. The observations were made on straight level sections of road away from junctions, and delays at intersections may have grown with the increase in traffic. Nevertheless it seems likely that, even before an extensive motorway system had been constructed, journey speeds were beginning to increase. One reason is that cars were able to travel faster as a result of improvements in the design and performance of vehicles.

Car ownership

Although it can scarcely be denied that there has been a considerable increase in mobility for the population as a whole, some argue that the benefits have been confined to a relatively narrow section of the community. Dr Mayer Hillman replies to the suggestion that most people have a car by saying that, even if this refers to household car ownership, it is incorrect, 'as about 45 per cent of households in Britain are without cars.'[7] This means that a clear majority of households *do own cars* and that Dr Hillman is talking nonsense unless he is able to show that families with cars are smaller than average. He makes no such attempt and even fails to distinguish between the proportion of households with cars and the proportion of the population in car-owning households.[8]

In reality households with cars are somewhat larger than average. In 1971, 51 per cent of households owned a car and these households accounted for 58 per cent of the population.[9] By 1975 the proportion of the population in car-owning households had increased to around 64 per cent and a further two per cent of families had a motorcycle or moped.[10]

Not only does the bulk of the population already live in households which have a car but the minority without one is also likely to get progressively smaller. The Department of the Environment expects the proportion of car-owning families to rise to 60 per cent by 1980 and 70 per cent by 1990.[11] The Department does not provide any estimate of the population they will contain. However if those families that become car owners by 1980 contain an average of 2.5 persons (the figure for all non-car-owning households in 1971) about two thirds of the population will by that date be in households with cars. And if families which still lack a motor in 1990 average two persons, around 80 per cent of the population will by then be in car-owning households. The Department, which is well aware that families without cars contain a disproportionate number of single-person households, is therefore being misleading when it declares in its **Consultation Document** that, 'even in the 1990s nearly one third of households will not own a car.'[12] What it should have said is that its estimates suggest that *by 1990* only about a fifth of the population will be in households without cars.

It should not be assumed that those who live in a non-car-owning household necessarily rely on public transport. Many live in households where, because of age and infirmity, virtually no use is made of public transport and some households without cars share houses with close relatives with cars.[13]

Have non-car owners become less mobile?

It may be argued that though a large and increasing majority of the population live in car-owning households, the minority is still important and that, to quote the Department of the Environment, 'mobility has been reduced for those without a car'.[14] The Department does not support this assertion with facts and figures and the available evidence suggests that there has been a striking increase in the mobility of households which do not own a car. Believers in a golden age before the working class began to buy cars would do well to look at the Ministry of Labour's family expenditure survey for 1937-38. The inquiry covered households headed by employed manual workers and by salaried employees who earned not more than £250 a year, the average salary.[15] The 10,396 households in the sample spent an average of only 3.39p per week on public transport, apart from journeys to and from work.[16] As the average charge on public transport was then about 0.325p per passenger mile, and the households contained an average of about 3.6 persons over the age of three, each travelled about three miles by public transport.[17]

It can be estimated from the National Travel Survey of 1965 that the 12,511 individuals over the age of three who lived in non-car-owning households travelled about $13\frac{1}{2}$ miles per week by rail, bus and coach, excluding journeys to and from work and in the course of work. In addition they travelled $6\frac{1}{2}$ miles by car.[18] A further survey in 1972-73 shows even higher figures, despite the large growth in car ownership which must have led to the removal from the non-car-owning category of those who tended to travel most. The 7,314 individuals in households without cars travelled about 15 miles by rail, bus and coach and another eight miles by car.[19] There can have been few opportunities for obtaining lifts before the war, so a fair comparison can probably be made between the three miles that members of working and lower middle class families travelled on public transport each week in 1937-38, for purposes other than work, with the 23 miles that those who belonged to non-car-owning households travelled by rail, bus, coach and car during 1972-73. This may underestimate the increase in mobility of those without cars: the most mobile sections of the working and lower middle class have purchased cars since 1937-38; and the National Travel Survey included the unemployed and the retired. These groups accounted for no less than 40 per cent of those households without cars.[20]

38

It is possible that although those without cars are more mobile now than in 1937-38 and 1965 they are less mobile than they were in the early 1950s, the heyday of public transport. At that time the passenger mileage by rail and on public service vehicles was around 75 billion. By 1973 the figure had fallen to 55.7 billion. However the decline in the passenger mileage by public transport, at 19-20 billion, is almost offest by the distance that those in non-car-owning households travelled by car during 1973, viz. 17.5 billion.[21] Since those who bought cars between the early fifties and 1973 must have covered fewer miles by public transport, it is difficult to avoid the conclusion that the passenger mileage of those who did not have a car in the early fifties and had not bought one by 1973 substantially increased.

Rural travel

There could nevertheless have been a decline in the mobility of those who live in rural areas because of the withdrawal of bus services. However, the level of car ownership is particularly high in the country. In 1971 only 26 per cent of those who lived in rural districts in England and Wales were in non-car-owning households and today the figure is probably only about 24 per cent.[22] Moreover the proportion appears to be especially low in those areas which are most isolated and where bus services are, and always have been, minimal. In villages which are not served by bus the proportion of households without cars is sometimes as low as ten per cent. The great bulk of the rural population therefore belong to car-owning households, and the spread of car ownership has almost certainly led to a large increase in mobility. In one area for which information is available – the district west of Crediton in Devon – the rise in car ownership from 44 per cent of households (in 1963) to 72 per cent (1971) was accompanied by an increase in the number of journeys made in a week from an average of 5.5 to 6.8 per person.[23]

It could still be true that the minority without cars are worse off. The Department of the Environment asserts that 'in country areas where public transport has been most extensively reduced the opportunities for mobility of people without access to a car are lower now than they have been for a generation or more.'[24] This seems far from certain. A survey of 5,796 inhabitants of 24 rural parishes in Devon and West Suffolk showed that in 1971 only six per cent of journeys were made on the local bus but that eight per cent took the form of lifts. It may be supposed that the low figure for bus journeys was due to the fact that services had already been drastically pruned. However, this does not seem to be the case, for in West Suffolk, where services had been maintained more or less intact and two thirds of the sample lived within five minutes of a bus stop, the proportion of journeys by bus was no higher than in Devon.[25]

It appeared that lifts were relatively easy to obtain, especially where the bus service was poor. In the Devon parishes, where only about a quarter of the people over 65 had cars, the official study group reported that 'where there is a good bus service (east of Tiverton) the elderly make slightly more journeys than average, i.e. they were more mobile, but not a lot more mobile. In other areas the relative frequency of bus services did not seem to make much difference to how often they travelled. In the areas worst served by buses, the survey showed that the elderly were able to get many lifts, and lifts formed a much larger proportion of their journeys than of those for other age groups. This suggests that relatives and friends are prepared to help out.'[26]

Have non-drivers become less mobile?
So far attention has been almost entirely confined to families without cars and no account has been taken of the possible reduction in the mobility of those in car-owning households who are not able to drive the car either because they cannot drive or because it is being used by somebody else. According to Dr Hillman, 'the implicit assumption of most planning studies that the "household" car necessarily enables all its members to be highly mobile runs counter to reality. Indeed it is debatable whether the gain to people in car-owning households who do not hold licences is out-weighed by the disadvantages of the decline in convenience of getting about by other means.'[27]

Some statistical light can be thrown on this possibility by subtracting the mileage that car drivers and motorcyclists drive themselves from total passenger mileage by private motorised transport. The results are shown within brackets in the Table. It can be seen that the residual mileage increased from 17 billion in 1953, to 62 billion in 1964 and 100 billion in 1973.[28] This exaggerates the growth in the mobility of those who are now driven because it does not allow for the mileage that they used to travel on public transport or bicycle. If, to take the extreme case, they accounted for all personal travel on bus and train, apart from journeys to work and school, their aggregate mileage in 1953 would only have amounted to something like 57 billion.[29] This is substantially less than the 70 billion miles that members of car-owning families were driven in 1973, excluding work and school journeys.[30] Yet it is obvious that the 1953 figure is much too high, if only because it includes the mileage that those from non-car-owning families travelled on public transport, while the 1973 figure is too low because it excludes the mileage that non-drivers travelled by public transport and bicycle despite the alleged reduction in their convenience due to the spread of car ownership. It seems, then, that there has been a very substantial increase in the mobility of those members of car-owning families who are unable to drive.

Some might object that the poor car driver has to spend a large part of his time ferrying other people about and that however mobile housewives may be at other times they are immobile during the day because husbands take cars to work or they themselves are unable to drive. 'Paradoxically', argues the gloomy Dr Hillman, 'when one is available, the mother often gets involved in acting as a chauffeur for the rest of the family. Nevertheless, few women who can drive have the use of the "family" car during the day.'[31] It seems that whatever happens all is for the worst in a car dependent world: either cars are not available and those without them are immobile, or they are available, which means that their drivers suffer the drudgery of chauffeuring! It would be wrong to exaggerate the extent of this activity. The National Travel Survey showed that in 1972-73 12 per cent of car drivers' mileage was for the purpose of carrying or accompanying some- body else, although the proportion rises to 21 per cent if journeys to work are excluded.[32] Moreover it is difficult to believe that driving children is regarded very differently by parents from those other jobs and duties – often pleasant, sometimes irksome and always time-consuming – that parents undertake for the good of their offspring. What is certain is that the availability of public transport has no bearing on the amount of chauffeuring in which many parents engage, for it appears that even by the age of ten only about half of all children are allowed to travel alone.[33]

There is considerably more truth in the contention that cars are taken to work and wives cannot drive. In 1972-73, 56 per cent of cars were used for work and only 28 per cent of those with full licences were women.[34] However, the pro- portion of households with a second car and the percentage of women that are able to drive are exceptionally high in areas where public transport is poor. Dr Hillman found that in a small Oxfordshire village which he investigated 45 per cent of housewives were able to drive, as against only 14 per cent in an inner London suburb.[35] In 1971, 19 per cent of the population in rural districts was in households with two or more cars compared with only 11 per cent in England and Wales as a whole.[36] It should also be remembered that the proportion of women drivers is rising and is likely to go on increasing.

Nevertheless there is no denying that housewives, even in car-owning house- holds, are likely to be relatively immobile during work hours. This does not mean that they are any less mobile than they have always been. As Dr Hillman has pointed out, travelling with young children on public transport is inconvenient and shopping by bus is particularly difficult with children.[37] What seems to happen in many households where the car is taken to work is that shopping and other trips which used to be made by wives during the week are now deferred to the weekend when a family expedition takes place. It would therefore be wrong, in the absence of any positive evidence of hardship, to conclude that the immobility of housewives during the working week is a matter for concern.

Social costs and summary

It is widely believed that the growth in road travel and traffic, besides its other adverse consequences, has also led to a steadily rising number of accidents and has had an increasingly harmful effect on the environment. During 1974, 6,880 people were killed on the roads. This was considerably less than in 1934, when there were 7,340 road deaths, but slightly more than the 6,650 which occurred in 1938. However, the population was considerably lower in 1938 and the rate per million was in fact somewhat higher than in 1974, viz. 144 as against 126 in 1974. In 1954 only 5,010 were killed and even the rate was, at 101, significantly less than in 1974. But in 1964 there were 7,820 road deaths, which was substantially more than in 1974.[38] Hence it is not true to say that there has been a steady increase in the number killed, although it is higher than it was in the 1950s. It is also worthy of note that deaths among pedestrians and cyclists – the groups which bear rather than inflict social costs – are now lower than at any time since 1934.[39] Very little information seems to be available on the way in which the environmental effects of road traffic have altered over time, but a recent study of traffic noise in London suggests that the situation is no worse than it was during the early sixties.

There has, to sum up, been a huge increase in the volume of travel during the postwar period and a marked improvement in its quality. These developments have been primarily due to the spread of car ownership, which has progressed to the point where a large majority of the population live in households that have a car. The improvement in mobility has not been confined to car drivers but has extended to other members of car-owning families, and the available evidence suggests that households without cars have also become more mobile. The increase in travel and traffic has not led to a reduction in car speeds, which have increased for inter-city journeys. Nor has it led to an ever increasing number of road deaths which, although they are higher now than they were in the 1950s, are lower than in the thirties and sixties.

1. PEP, *Personal Mobility and Transport Policy*, Broadsheet, No. 542, June 1973, p. 21.
2. Ibid., p. 23.
3. Richard Pryke and Leonard Tivey, Memorandum in Select Committee on Nationalised Industries, *Relations with the Public*, House of Commons Paper 514 of 1970-71, pp. 525-27.
4. Road Research Laboratory, *Research on Road Traffic*, HMSO, 1965, pp. 239-43; T. M. Coburn, Trends in Speeds on British Main Roads, in *Proceedings of the third Conference of the Australian Road Research Board*, 1966, Vol. 3. Part 1, pp. 600, 601; Department of the Environment (henceforth referred to as DoE), *Transport policy: A Consultation Document*,

HMSO, 1976, Vol. 2, p. 58.
5. Road Research Laboratory, op. cit., p. 112.
6. Coburn, op. cit., pp. 594-96, 601, 602.
7. PEP, op. cit., pp. 75, 76.
8. Ibid., pp. 76, 77.
9. Office of Population Censuses and Surveys, *Census 1971 England and Wales: Availability of Cars*, HMSO, 1973, Table 1. General Register Office Edinburgh, *Census 1971 Scotland: Housing Report*, HMSO, 1975, Table 20.
10. Department of Employment, *Family Expenditure Survey 1975*, HMSO, 1976, Table 70; DoE, *National Travel Survey 1972-73*, HMSO, 1975, Table 1.
11. DoE. *Transport Policy : A Consultation Document*, Vol. 1, p. 4.
12. Ibid., p. 12.

42

13. Seven and a half per cent of the households covered by the National Travel Survey of 1972-73 did not undertake any journey of more than a mile during the sample week (DoE, *National Travel Survey 1972-73,* Table 6). Some of these households may have had their mobility restricted by illness during the survey week, but there would have been others where the only journey of more than a mile was by foot.
14. DoE, op. cit., p. 12.
15. *Ministry of Labour Gazette,* December 1940, p. 300; Dudley Seers, *The Levelling of Incomes Since 1938,* Basil Blackwell, p. 51.
16. *Gazette,* December 1940, pp. 300, 301, 305, January 1941, p. 11.
17. Richard Stone and D. A. Rowe, *The Measurement of Consumers' Expenditure and Behaviour in the United Kingdom 1920-1938,* Vol. 2, pp. 71,72; *Gazette,* December 1940, p. 304, January 1941, p. 10.
18. Ministry of Transport, *Passenger Transport in Great Britain 1967,* HMSO, 1969, Tables 10, 12; information from DoE.
19. DoE, *National Travel Survey 1972-73,* Table 27; information from DoE.
20. DoE, op. cit., Table 2.
21. Ibid., Tables 26, 27; text Table.
22. Office of Population Censuses and Surveys, op. cit., Table 1; DoE. *Transport Policy; A Consultation Document,* Vol. 1, p. 36.
23. DoE, *Study of Rural Transport in Devon: Report by the Steering Group,* unpublished, pp. 5, 25, (henceforth this and the companion study on West Suffolk will be referred to as Rural Transport in Devon/West Suffolk).
24. DoE, *Transport Policy: A Consultation Document,* Vol. 1, p. 12.
25. DoE, *Rural Transport in West Suffolk,* pp. 2, 22-24, 29; *Rural Transport in Devon,* p. 24.
26. DoE, *Rural Transport in Devon,* pp. 8, 9.
27. PEP, op. cit., p. 79.
28. These figures must only be regarded as approximations as the data on which they are based are both crude and limited, especially in the case of vehicle occupancy.
29. Text table; Ministry of Labour and National Service, *Report of an Enquiry into Household Expenditure in 1953-54,* HMSO, 1957, p.235; Ministry of Transport, *Passenger Transport in Great Britain 1963,* HMSO, 1965, Tables 3, 6, 37.
30. DoE, *National Travel Survey 1972-73,* Tables 26, 27, *Passenger Transport in Great Britain 1973,* Table 1.
31. PEP, op. cit., p. 11.
32. Information from DoE.
33. PEP, op. cit., p. 68.
34. DoE. *National Travel Survey 1972-73,* Table 13, information from DoE.
35. PEP, op. cit., p. 55.
36. Office of Population Censuses and Surveys, op. cit., Table 1.
37. PEP, op. cit., p. 11.
38. DoE, Scottish Development Department and Welsh Office, *Road Accidents 1969,* HMSO, 1971, Table 1; British Road Federation, *Basic Road Statistics 1975,* Table 9. Deaths have been rounded to the nearest ten.
39. British Road Federation, op. cit., Table 9; Central Statistical Office, *Annual Abstract of Statistics No. 84, 1935-1946,* HMSO, 1948, Table 232.

A REJOINDER

Mayer Hillman and Anne Whalley

In attempting to assess the changes in mobility that have occurred in the last 30 or 40 years, Dr Pryke refers extensively and critically to PEP's research on this subject, and particularly to *Personal Mobility and Transport Policy*. His quotations from this book are selective and misleading, and he paraphrases in a manner which distorts their original meaning.[1]

Within this context, we feel obliged to react to his paper on two crucial aspects of transport policy. Firstly his view of mobility and secondly the apparent presumption that if substantial change to policy is needed, the change is not deemed necessary for hardship or other social considerations.

Dr Pryke takes issue with the contention that 'the benefits of increasing mobility have accrued to only a relatively small section of the population'. He commits the cardinal error of so many transport experts (including the authors of the Government's current Consultation Document on Transport Policy), of overlooking the significance of *walking* in the daily travel of the population at large, and especially of course of those without access to a car. Without doubt, the convenience of walking and the quality of the pedestrian environment have generally declined over the years, owing to the substantial rise in traffic volumes, particularly freight. In addition planning changes and locational decisions have resulted in people having to walk further or, indeed, in destinations no longer being accessible on foot.

Throughout his paper, Dr Pryke makes it clear that his measure of mobility largely stems from establishing the motorised mileage that people travel. As a consequence of this and his analysis of transport statistics, he concludes that people in car-owning *and* non-car-owning households have experienced an increase in their mobility in postwar years. We consider that the motorised mileage that people travel is not necessarily a reflection of mobility and that many of the benefits of 'the huge increase in the volume of travel' are doubtful: for example, longer journeys entailed by the closure of local shops or schools, or by their scaling up in newer developments, could hardly be interpreted, even by an economist, as a mobility benefit.

To take the population in car-owning households first,[2] we agree that those who do not have their own car derive mobility benefits from the household car, just as Dr Pryke agrees that this car is not necessarily available all the time, that for many travel by it entails making sure that a driver is also available, and that this can result in a loss of independence for both parties involved. Where we do part company with him is in our relative assessment of the acceptability of this state of affairs. He interprets our arguments in a rather jocular way as indicating that you can't win because of the identified disbenefits, whereas we interpret them as indicating the need for a radical change in policy so that these disbenefits would be far less likely to be incurred.

In spite of his criticisms therefore we still maintain the belief that in car-owning households those without their own car have on balance become worse off in mobility terms (particularly of course relative to those with a car of their own).

Our comments both on the significance of walking, and on the inappropriateness of motorised mileage as a measure of mobility, are even more relevant to people in non-car-owning households. Indeed, in our view, their increased public transport mileage might, as indicated earlier, in many instances reflect not travel choice so much as travel necessity brought about by planning changes and new developments. Unfortunately, it is very difficult to ascertain how much of the increase is brought about by the fact that trips on foot are no longer possible. Indeed this could well be the reason also for the apparently increasing number of journeys in the DoE rural transport study cited by Dr Pryke, for this study excluded journeys of under one mile – that is the great majority of walk trips.

Where public transport is relevant to mobility, however, it is not the mileage travelled but the *availability* of the service – even more than its *quality*. In suggesting that people without access to cars are not really worse off nowadays, Dr Pryke seems unaware of the decline in public transport, some of the features of which are illustrated in the table on the following page.

This decline has in fact been even more marked than the table would at first suggest for the residential areas that public transport has to serve are now spread over a much larger acreage than they were twenty years ago. We doubt whether those people whose public transport services have been curtailed or cut, or their travel made dependent on interchange, would agree with Dr Pryke that the quality of services has improved, albeit that Inter-City services are faster and more comfortable and some routes have been electrified.

The table also shows how relatively greater has been the cost of public transport travel, on a declining public transport system, compared with the cost of car travel on an expanding road system. Indeed, relative to total consumers' expenditure, the cost of public transport travel has risen whereas that of car travel has declined.

There are two other issues about which we find Dr Pryke too complacent. He

Changes in Transport Services and Costs, 1953/4 to 1974

	1954	1964	1974	% change 1954-74
British Rail:				
route miles	19,151	11,670	8,931	− 53%
passenger stations	5,746	3,574	2,355	− 59%
passenger trains (million loaded miles)	229.5	209.5	185.5	− 19%
passenger receipts (estimated average per passenger mile) new pence	0.56	0.83	1.71	+ 205%
Road Public Transport:				
public service vehicles	80,643	76,979	77,363	− 4%
p.s.v. miles (million	2,499	2,358	2,151	− 14%
index of stage service fares	100	170	381	+ 281%
Road Private Transport:				
motorway mileage	0	292	1,108	∞
trunk roads	8,270	8,336	8,358	+ 1%
other roads (1000 miles)	179	191	204	+ 14%
Passenger Transport, cost to consumer:	1953	1964	1974	
index of rail fares	100	173	353	
index of p.s.v. fares	100	173	374	
index of car prices[1]	100	94	150	
index of vehicle running cost	100	116	242	
index of expenditure on all goods and services	100	131	251	

[1] new and secondhand, including motor cycles

cites the fact that, in London, traffic noise is 'no worse that it was during the early 1960s', confirming that it was bad then, and implying that we do not need to be *too* concerned about it now. We doubt whether the many Londoners in the survey in question who reported high levels of noise would agree. And we are not sure to whom he refers in stating that 'it is widely believed that the growth in road travel and traffic . . . has led to a steadily rising number of accidents'. We know of *no one* who thinks so, but we are nonetheless concerned about its scale. More seriously we take exception to this callous attitude to road accidents. As with his comments on noise, he implies that the continuing toll of about 7,000 road deaths per annum – or over a quarter of a million in his lifetime – is acceptable. Moreover, he neglects to comment on the far higher numbers of people seriously injured.

Finally, we wish to add that Dr Pryke appears to identify those groups with

46

whom he disagrees as all favouring the same policies. Hence, after attempting to dismiss our interpretation of the realities of transport, he states – 'This means that the underlying assumptions of those who advocate massive subsidies for public transport are incorrect'. However, although we do believe our assumptions to be right, we do not use the conclusions we draw from them to recommend large subsidies for public transport. Indeed, it is rather ironical that we share with Dr Pryke many of the views expressed in his following paper about the inadequate costing to the public of both private and public transport travel.

1. For instance, we did not state that cycling is 'an inferior mode' nor could it be construed from the diagrams or text, but we realistically pointed out that it cannot match the speed of the car over longer distances. And he finds fault with us because we dislike the word 'majority' being used to refer to 55 per cent of car-owning households. (He fails to mention that we object to the use of the term 'universal' car ownership as a description of the same 55 per cent of households.) Of course he is technically correct, though the use he makes of comparable terms in his paper is far more sus-

pect: he cites 45 per cent of licence-holding housewives in our rural survey as 'exceptionally high'. We wonder what phraseology he would use to describe the level of licence holding among their husbands – which is twice as high.

2. We acknowledge the error in the diagram to which he refers, though it is small and not very relevant to our general thesis.

3. Mayer Hillman and Anne Whalley, 'Land Use and Travel', *Built Environment Quarterly,* September, 1975, pp. 105-111.

THE CASE AGAINST SUBSIDIES
Richard Pryke

The extent of subsidy

If a policy of subsidy were the answer to our transport problems they would already have been solved, as public transport now receives large-scale financial assistance. The precise sum that is received in subsidies is of no great interest because it depends, among other things, on the extent to which capital has been written off and provided free of charge. What is economically relevant is the size of the gap between the revenue that bus and railway undertakings earn and the value of the resources that they use.

In principle the fuel and licence duties that bus operators pay, or at least would pay but for the fuel grants, should be disregarded because they are a transfer and not a payment for resources used. However, in practice they can be regarded as a payment towards the cost of providing and maintaining the road system. According to the DoE's estimates the fuel and licence duties paid by buses and coaches are, at £53 million in 1975-6, not very different from that part of public road costs that can be attributed to buses and coaches, at £65 million.[1] Hence in the Table, which shows the revenue and expenditure of the major passenger transport operators, fuel and excise duties have been treated as a resource cost.

Since bygones are bygones, depreciation on past investment should in principle be ignored, and the amount that BR and some of the bus operators set aside is grossly inadequate, if only because it is calculated at historic cost. In the absence of any better figure investment during the years under consideration has been regarded as the quantity of capital used in the process of production. This would be unsatisfactory if traffic were growing rapidly and large amounts of extra equipment were required, or if investment fluctuated widely from year to year, and is considerably above its average level. However, this is not the case, and undertakings will therefore need to earn enough to cover their investment even if they are to do no more than recover the capital resources that they employ.[2]

In 1975 none of the main passenger transport undertakings earned enough to meet even their current operating costs. The Scottish Transport Group's buses came nearest. They had a deficit of £6 million and their expenditure exceeded

**Earnings and Expenditure of Principal Public
Transport Operators, 1975 (£m.)**

	British Rail		London Transport		National Bus Company	Scottish Bus Group	Passenger Transport Executives
	Passenger	Total	Road	Rail			
Expenditure							
before depreciation	748	1,184	166	122	302	61	215
Bus fuel grant	–	–	5	–	14	3	10
Total operating costs	748	1,184	171	122	316	64	225
Earnings	454	831	81*	100	293†	58*	135*
Current deficit	294	353	90	22	23	6	90
Capital expenditure	..	108	13	43	24	6	25
	..	461	103	65	48	12	115

* Excludes grants in respect of concessionary fare schemes.

† Includes grants in respect of concessionary fare schemes (£13 million in 1974).

Note the figures for the whole of British Rail's operations include receipts and expenditure from catering, advertising, operational property and BREL's external operations. The scope of the passenger figures, which are taken direct from BR's Annual Report (1975, p.8), is unclear. The PTE figures are only approximate.

their revenue by only eleven per cent. At the other end of the spectrum of unprofitability were London Transport's buses which lost £90 million, and where current costs were well over twice as great as revenue. Between the two extremes came London Underground, the Passenger Transport Executives, the National Bus Company and British Rail's passenger services. The latter recorded a loss of £295 million, which was the largest absolute amount and meant that costs were 65 per cent greater than earnings. In all, these public transport operators had a current deficit of about £540 million and if BR's freight deficit is included the figure was around £600 million.

As the capital expenditure of these undertakings amounted to £220 million (including perforce the whole of BR's investment) their total resource deficit was £820 million; and their expenditure, both capital and current, exceeded their commercial revenue by around 55 per cent. Even the nationalised bus companies, where the financial problem was at its least serious, had a resource deficit of about £75 million, which represented about 22 per cent of revenue. BR failed to cover its costs by £460 million (55 per cent of revenue); the underground had a resource loss of £65 million (65 per cent); the PTEs had one of £115 million (85 per cent); and the London buses had a resource deficit of over £100 million (equivalent to over 125 per cent of what they earned).

Railways: A cautionary tale

One reason why subsidies escalate is that they lead to a loss of control over costs, as the railways' recent history illustrates. Over the period 1963-69 BR made large gains in efficiency and there was an increase of 43 per cent in labour productivity. However, since then very little progress has been made and during 1974 productivity was only one and a half per cent greater than it had been in 1969. The gains in efficiency during the sixties were largely due to the switch from steam to diesel and electric traction and to the programme of rational-isation launched by Dr Beeching. By 1969 steam had been eliminated and some of the most obvious economies had already been made.[3]

Nevertheless BR had considerable scope for saving labour and raising productivity. Financial forecasts which the Board prepared in 1967 appear to have been based on the assumption that the rail labour force would be reduced to no more than 200,000 in 1974, including Freightliners.[4] At the end of 1969 a new estimate of future manpower requirements prepared by BR's work study staff showed that the work force could be slimmed down to 201,000. At the end of 1974 BR still had 233,000 workers.

The underlying reason why costs were not reduced was almost certainly the 1968 Transport Act. The financial arrangements which it embodied were re-garded by the Government as a full, fair and final settlement of the railways' claim for assistance. However according to Dr Stewart Joy, who was closely involved in the work of the Joint Steering Group that preceded the Act, the most common attitude of the BR representatives was that 'its purpose was to "white-wash the deficit" '.[5] This is confirmed by others involved in the Steering Group. Moreover, the Transport Act had scarcely taken effect before BR's chairman was calling for freight subsidies. The moral which the Board drew from the Act was that if the Government were prepared, virtually without question, to sub-sidise those parts of the system where traffic was sparse and costs greatly exceeded revenue, it would support the main lines if they too became unprofit-able.

This view was correct for in 1973 the Government decided to abandon the 1968 Transport Act and to introduce a general passenger subsidy. As a result BR was under virtually no pressure to control its costs and, despite the fall in traffic, increased its employment from 223,000 at the end of 1973 to 231,000 in March 1975 by means of a vigorous recruitment drive.[6] At about this time the Board was informed that there must be no further increase in the passenger subsidy and that it must eliminate its freight deficit. As a result recruitment was brought under control and within thirteen months employment had, without pain or protest, been cut by about 9,000 through natural wastage.

The Board is also now proposing to make a slightly greater saving in man-power by 1981 than had previously been planned. The announced intention had been to reduce the rail labour force to 190,000 by 1981. Because of pressure from the Government, BR is now planning to cut staff to 182,000 and has at last declared that guards are unnecessary where passenger trains have power doors and freight trains have continuous brakes, although it is wrongly arguing that extensive investment is necessary before these changes are introduced. My detailed estimates, when put on the same basis as the Board's, suggest that by 1981 BR could slim down its employment by a further 25,000 to about 157,000.[7] British Rail could make a larger saving than it is planning by removing firemen, now politely termed second men, from diesel and electric trains – a development which has already taken place in Holland. (Instead it is placing co-drivers on its high-speed trains although they were originally designed for single manning.) It also seems clear that large additional savings in drivers could be made by increasing the time that they actually drive from the present level of about 3.75 hours per turn of duty and by raising the speed of freight trains, which now only average some 22.5 mph. Further economies in manpower over and above those for which BR allowed could be made by introducing automatic barriers at suburban stations and by confining Inter-City ticket checking to the train. In this way large numbers of platform staff could be dispensed with.

Not only is BR planning to employ far more staff than it needs but it also wants to carry out a large amount of unnecessary investment. Between 1968 and 1972 its capital expenditure averaged about £140 million a year, at 1975 purchasing power. In 1972 the Board appears to have told the Department that an annual investment of around £215 million was necessary over the period 1973-81. However in its Interim Strategy of 1973 the Board stepped up its programme to £320 million because financial discipline had relaxed and it believed that the political climate was favourable. Initially the government sanctioned a level of capital expenditure that was only a little lower, but the figure has been progressively cut back to about £275 million at 1975 purchasing power. However this is still well above the £205 million a year which a detailed investigation shows is the most than can be justified, or that is necessary if BR is to carry the traffic that is likely to be available.[8]

The moral to be drawn from this cautionary tale is that subsidies, by undermining financial discipline, blunt the incentive to cut costs and encourage wasteful investment. Moreover foreign experience shows that rail subsidies have been escalating in an apparently uncontrollable fashion almost everywhere that public assistance has been provided.[9] Unfortunately the inflationary effect which subsidy has on both current and capital expenditure is virtually ignored by those who advocate the provision of financial support for public transport on welfare grounds. This is partly because economists customarily assume that undertakings operate on the lowest possible cost curves, and partly because of the difficulty of making any quantitative allowance for greater inefficiency in cost-benefit calculations. However the main reason is probably the feeling that excess costs can be avoided if only suitable control mechanisms can be devised. This is almost certainly a delusion. The 1968 Transport Act was an elaborate and well thought out attempt to provide a restricted subsidy which would not impair but would actually promote efficiency. It failed dismally and within a very short space of time.

The costs and benefits of subsidies

Insofar as subsidies cause inefficiency (i.e. cause costs at any level of output to be higher than they would otherwise have been), that is a source of social loss. It could happen that the decrease in efficiency was so great that the railways (or buses) could not, despite the subsidy, make any reduction in their charges. The whole subsidy would then be a social loss.

Consider, however, the case where the decrease in efficiency is less than that, so that some reduction in charges *is* made. What are the social pluses and minuses to be set alongside whatever loss is due to decreased efficiency?

There will be some switch of traffic from private to public transport. This is held to be desirable, by those who support subsidies, for the following reason. The optimum output of any product or service is at the point where the marginal social cost is equal to the marginal social benefit. In other words, where a small increase in output will impose greater costs on society than the extra benefits that it confers, but where if a small reduction is made benefits will exceed costs. The actual output will be where the marginal private cost is equal to the marginal private benefit, i.e. consumers will go on buying any given commodity until the additional benefit they obtain is just equal to the price that they have to pay. In the case of cars, it is argued that there is a divergence between private and social cost, (a) because cars cause noise and other disamenities for which the driver is not charged, and (b) because, if on any road traffic has increased to the point where congestion is occurring, the presence of an extra car will slow down other road users. Since time has a value, this means that a social cost is being imposed. Hence car usage may be above optimum. Railways do not usually inflict any costs on society over and above the cost of the resources they employ in providing their services, although the presence of extra passengers on rush hour trains that are already crowded will reduce the welfare of those who have already boarded. Hence it is argued that if traffic is shifted from road to rail this will bring the transport system nearer the optimum. If road passenger transport is subsidised and more buses have to be run, in order to accommodate the extra passengers, congestion will be caused. However the social costs per passenger mile are likely to be comparatively light because buses have a large carrying capacity in relation to their size.

This argument for subsidising public transport is true as far as it goes. However what it ignores, besides the pure inefficiency that may arise, is that although subsidies will lead to some movement towards the optimum use of cars there will be a movement away from the optimum for public transport. Because of the subsidies bus and rail services are being supplied at a price which does not fully reflect the cost of the resources they use. Hence the welfare of society is reduced by an amount equivalent to such part of the cost of carrying the extra bus and rail passengers which they would not be willing to pay because they do not value the service sufficiently highly. As a result the net benefit which subsidies provide will always be smaller than it appears and, if the loss of welfare in public transport is sufficiently large, society may, on balance, be worse off. This is a point which those who advocate subsidies often ignore because, owing to their preoccupation with environmental effects, they forget that the resources that public transport employs are a relevant social cost.

There will also be a movement away from the optimum and a loss of welfare as a result of taxes levied to meet the cost of the subsidy. If indirect taxation is raised the prices of the goods involved will be raised above their costs of production. As a result their output will now tend to be suboptimal and part or all of the gain in welfare from subsidising public transport will be lost. Similar arguments apply if the Government raises direct taxation, while if it cuts other public expenditure the community will lose the benefits of those items that are sacrificed.

Whether despite these adverse consequences the welfare of the community would, on balance, be improved by subsidies depends, among other things, on the extent to which prices diverge from social costs in public and private transport. If the divergence is large for private transport but small for public transport there could be a case for increasing subsidies whereas, if the divergence is larger for public transport, subsidies should be reduced. As we have seen there is likely to be a gap between private and social costs in road transport. It should be borne in mind that, by taxing petrol and diesel, the Government makes what amounts to a charge for the road system, and that the revenue it receives from motorists exceeds their share of the cost of providing and maintaining the road system. To this extent the difference between the price that motorists pay (i.e. their private costs) and the social costs they inflict is smaller than it appears although, as we shall see later, this is not the end of the story. However, the crucial point is that public transport is now incurring enormous losses, and is already receiving huge subsidies. This means that there is a large gap between the price that public transport users pay and the resource cost of providing the services. It is therefore difficult to believe that the divergence between prices and social costs is greater for private than for public transport. On the contrary it is almost certainly smaller and it follows that the community would be better off if subsidies were reduced.

There is a further reason why the welfare loss due to subsidising public transport is almost bound to outweigh the benefit when cars are used less. This is that lower fares are unlikely to cause any great shift from private to public transport, and most of the increase in bus and rail traffic will probably represent journeys that would not previously have been made, or would have been shorter. Obviously these journeys, since they have been generated and not diverted, will not produce any benefit in the form of reduced road congestion and noise. On the contrary they will, in so far as extra buses are required, tend to make the situation worse. Moreover rail subsidies will have an adverse effect on the environment by stimulating long distance commuting: urban sprawl will be more difficult to contain and it will be harder to reverse the decay of inner-city areas. Even if these disbenefits can somehow be avoided there will certainly be no gain to set against the welfare loss because public transport is being supplied at less than it costs to provide.

This point can be illustrated by means of a supply and demand diagram for a hypothetical public transport undertaking. It will be seen that its cost curve is

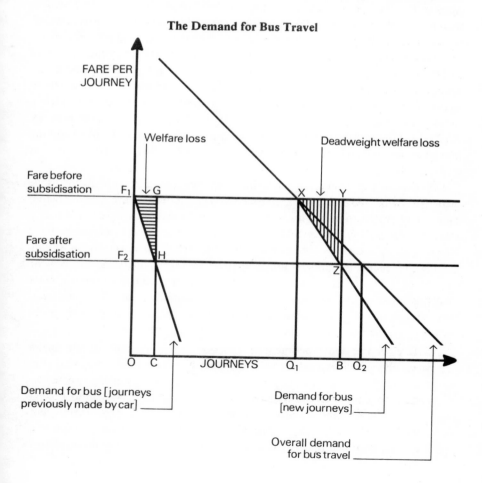

The Demand for Bus Travel

horizontal which implies that there are no economies or diseconomies of scale. This is not an essential assumption but simplifies the analysis.[10] In practice long-run cost curves seem to be more or less flat in the bus industry and henceforth the concern will be regarded as a bus company. It will also be assumed, again for purposes of exposition, that the company is initially just covering its costs although this is an unrealistic assumption.[11]

Besides the overall demand curve for bus travel, separate curves have been drawn for those journeys that prior to the subsidy were made by car and for all other journeys. When, because of the subsidy, fares are reduced from F_1 to F_2, OC journeys which car drivers used to make will now be undertaken by bus. But some entirely new journeys will also be made and some car passengers will switch to bus. These are indicated by the distance Q_1B. As a result the total number of journeys will increase from Q_1 to Q_2, where the distance BQ_2 is equal to OC, i.e. the number of journeys that car drivers previously made. The welfare loss when they transfer to bus is measured by the triangle F_1GH which is the amount by which the extra costs that the bus undertaking incurs (F_1GCO) exceed the total sum that the former car drivers are prepared to pay (F_1HCO). Fortunately, there will, as we have seen, be some welfare gain to set against this welfare loss because of the reduction in road traffic. However, there will be no such benefit in the case of those journeys that are entirely new. Hence the welfare loss sustained on these trips is deadweight. It is represented by XYZ, the difference between the extra costs that are inflicted ($XYBQ_1$) and the maximum amount that bus users would be prepared to pay for the journeys in question ($XZBQ_1$).

The available evidence suggests that very few car users are likely to be attracted if bus and rail fares are reduced. When motorists are asked whether they would switch to public transport if large fare reductions were made only a small proportion say they would, and empirical research on transport patterns also suggests that there would be relatively little effect.[12] However, the most convincing evidence that drivers are insensitive to fare reductions comes from various experiments that have been carried out. In a recent German scheme involving about 10,000 employees, the cost of a monthly public transport ticket was reduced by two thirds or more.[13] It was found that only 13 per cent of the workers switched to public transport. According to the DoE:

> A fares concession experiment in Tyneside, where a sample of households were given half price bus passes, showed that bus use increased only marginally, and car use declined very little. While this study, which was subject to a number of experimental problems, cannot be held to be conclusive, the closely monitored Stevenage 'Superbus' experiment yields similar results. In this experiment successive improvements to a neighbourhood to town centre bus route were introduced over a period of about a

year. The improvements were broadly a 50 per cent reduction in bus fares, doubled bus frequencies, together with faster journey times and more attractive buses. Although bus patronage rose significantly (nevertheless resulting in a considerable operating loss), only a small number of car driver commuters in the route's catchment area switched to the 'Superbus' service. The effect on car passengers was more marked, but . . . congestion is not reduced by reducing car occupancy rates.[14]

It might be true that although relatively few motorists transfer when fares are reduced they represent a high proportion of what little traffic is attracted. If it were the case it is by no means clear that it would make subsidisation more attractive. It would, of course, reduce the deadweight welfare loss that is sustained on that part of the additional passenger traffic which has not been diverted from cars but is newly generated, viz. XYZ in the diagram. But the fact that the demand for public transport in urban areas only increases by around 0.4 per cent for every one per cent by which prices are reduced means that a very heavy subsidy is necessary to secure any perceptible shift of traffic from car to bus and train, even if the bulk of the traffic is diverted from private transport.[15] Large-scale subsidisation means that there will almost certainly be a reduction in the efficiency with which public transport is operated and that a considerable amount of public money and scarce resources will therefore be wasted. Moreover, in order to pay the subsidy a large amount of extra taxation will have to be imposed or public expenditure will have to be sacrificed elsewhere.

In view of the welfare loss which taxation involves, the constraints on taxation and public expenditure and the way in which spending of a highly desirable type is now being sacrificed, it is difficult to believe that large low-yield subsidies to public transport can be justified.

A social service for the poor?

Some may say that public transport is a social service and as such deserves to be subsidised. Almost anything can be termed a social service and those who so describe buses and trains scarcely ever try to explain what they mean. I suspect that all too often they do not have anything in mind and that they are merely uttering incantations and repeating shibboleths. However what is presumably being asserted is that public transport is 'necessary' and 'essential'. A wide range of industries and products can plausibly be regarded as essential public services including undertaking, milk distribution, the baking of bread and the manufacture of childrens' clothing. Why should public transport be accorded priority? The contention that fare increases cause hardship has any substance only if expenditure on public transport represents a large proportion of the incomes of the poorest members of the community, while any hardship that would arise if services were withdrawn is only relevant to the argument where it is clear that the services cannot survive without subsidies. In 1971, before the wide-spread introduction of concessionary fare schemes, the 20 per cent of house-holds with the lowest incomes devoted only two per cent of their expenditure to public transport.[16] Thus the argument that higher fares cause hardship has very little force.

It is even doubtful whether subsidising public transport serves to redistribute income. The financial assistance that railways receive almost certainly has a perverse effect because the most affluent sections of the community account for an unusually high proportion of expenditure. In 1972-73, 48 per cent of per-sonal spending on rail travel came from the 20 per cent of households who were best off, though their share of all personal income was only 38 per cent.[17] On the other hand, those non-pensioner households that came within the richest 20 per cent accounted for 18 per cent of all (non-pensioner) expenditure on buses, which was much less than the 39 per cent of non-pensioner income which they commanded. Moreover, these non-pensioner households that were included in the poorest 40 per cent were responsible for 30 per cent of expenditure as against 15 per cent of all (non-pensioner) income.[18] This may give an exag-gerated impression of the extent to which the present bus subsidies redistribute income. London Transport buses incur a high proportion of the bus industry's overall deficit, but in the London area the top 20 per cent account for 36 per cent of all expenditure on buses.[19] Whatever assumptions are made, concessionary schemes for pensioners must, granted the bus industry's present pricing policies, be markedly egalitarian.

It seems likely however that the existing pricing structure is wrong because no differentiation is made between peak and off-peak journeys. Yet the latter appear to involve relatively little cost because of the existence of spare capacity, and concessionary schemes are often justified on the grounds that they help to fill empty seats.[20] What therefore seems desirable is that bus undertakings should charge a higher fare at peak periods than at other times but should withdraw concessionary fares. This would have the advantage that resources would be better allocated because it would discourage travel when buses are crowded and provide a general encouragement when there are plenty of spare seats. In those places where pensioners are permitted to travel free, and where the conces-sionary scheme is not restricted to off-peak periods, they would be worse off but where this happens resources are being misallocated. Moreover pensioners who have the misfortune to live in local authority areas where no scheme has been introduced would be better off as the public money that is saved could be returned to old age pensioners in other ways.

The most desirable of these is an increase in pensions or supplementary benefits. This would enable their recipients to spend the money in the way that gives them the greatest satisfaction. Why, as at present, should we give preferential treatment to those who are able and willing to travel by bus but refuse to assist those who would, for instance, prefer a telephone? As Dr Mayer Hillman points out, 'both old and severely disabled people can benefit from owning a telephone, although only a small proportion have one. It can provide a substitute for physical mobility; for example it can be used to keep in touch with others who have one, and as an alternative way of shopping by ordering goods for delivery'.[21]

There is a general point here. The problem with the poor is not that they cannot afford those items that politicians, officials and the well-meaning believe that they need, but that they have insufficient money to spend in such a way as to yield them the greatest possible satisfaction.[22] Hence even where support for public transport has a favourable effect on the distribution of income, as it probably does in the case of bus subsidies, I believe that it is preferable to use the funds for increasing old age pensions, family allowances and other cash benefits. At this point those who are convinced that public transport should be subsidised will argue that the money being used to assist public transport is insufficient to have a perceptible effect on the distribution of income. If this is so, subsidies can scarcely be defended on distributional grounds. The argument is moreover a very lame one in view of the enormous resources with which public transport is being transfused.

Road taxation

If it is true, as the proponents of subsidies suppose, that car users do not meet the full costs that they impose on society one possible solution is to alter the level and reform the structure of motor taxation. But is it true? It is estimated by the Department of the Environment that during 1975-76 private motorists contributed £1,535 million to government revenue in the form of fuel tax (£700 million); the VAT paid on fuel which arises because it is taxed at more than the standard rate (£310 million); payments for licences (£400 million); and the tax that is paid on new cars (£125 million).[23] However, car tax and licence payments should be disregarded because, once a family has decided to buy and use a car, there is no variation in the amount that has to be paid. Hence these taxes have little or no effect on the amount that vehicles are used. They might influence the decision whether to acquire a car but not to any great extent because they make up only a small part of the total cost of motoring. Fuel taxation alone has any real effect on the volume of traffic. In 1975-76 private motorists appear to have paid £1,010 million of taxation on fuel, including the supplementary VAT element.

The Department estimates that expenditure out of public funds on their behalf to provide, maintain, light and police the road system came to £720 million.[24] At first sight it therefore appears that private motorists pay more than enough in taxation. However, no account has been taken of the fact that car users mis-perceive their expenditure. Various studies have shown that they tend to confine their attention to their out-of-pocket expenditure on fuel and ignore those other costs which vary with the distance travelled, namely expenditure on tyres, repair and maintenance, and mileage-related depreciation.[25] In 1974 personal ex-penditure on spare parts and the maintenance and repair of vehicles was about £1,020 million at 1975-76 purchasing power.[26] To bring home to motorists the expense they are incurring the government should increase fuel taxation until the net revenue that it obtains from the private car user approaches this sum.

During 1975-76 the fuel tax they paid (at £1,010 million) exceeded the public costs for which they are responsible (at £720 million) by only £290 million. If the government were to obtain a net revenue of £1,020 million it would be necessary to raise an extra £730 million in fuel taxation. Since private motorists spent £2,190 million on fuel and oil during 1974, at 1975-76 purchasing power, this would imply an increase of at least a third in the price of petrol.[27] How-ever the increase could and should be partly offset by the removal of car tax and the discontinuation of car licences (at least from their revenue-earning role).

Not only do motorists underestimate the expenditure they incur but they also inflict heavy costs on the community over and above those of providing and maintaining the road system. The quantification and treatment of these costs (which include accidents, noise and fumes) raises a number of problems that cannot be pursued in detail here. However, the correct approach is first to reduce the extent of the costs by making any changes in vehicle design and testing which cost-benefit analysis and common sense indicate are desirable. In this way it may, for instance, be possible partly to solve the problem of noise and fumes. The remaining costs can then be quantified. An estimate can be made from the cost of soundproofing those houses which are badly affected by noise, and grants should be available to help their occupants to pay for the necessary work. Much effort has been devoted to measuring the cost of road accidents and the Consultation Document puts the figure at £875 million in 1974, at 1975-76 prices.[28]

However, the Department asserts that a large part of this cost is borne by road users and can therefore be ignored. The argument for this is presumably that, since road users are prepared to run the risk of being involved in a road accident, we should be charging them twice if we tried to cover in taxation the share of the cost which they willingly bear. Such an attempt would be like taxing food on the ground that some people overeat and that this leads to heavy costs in the form of avoidable illness and premature death. It is an argument with considerable force, but it ignores the possibility that road users (or those who overeat) may underrate the risk they are running and that the consequences of an accident may be less serious for some types of road user than for others. When two cars crash the risks to each are more or less equal and they will, if drivers perceive them correctly, be taken into account by motorists. However, if a car is involved in an accident with a pedestrian, the latter is far more likely to pay the price, and car drivers will tend to ignore the costs to which their presence on the roads gives rise. If these costs are recovered by means of fuel taxation, car mileage will tend to decline and perhaps there will be some reduction in accidents. It would be appropriate for motorists to make a contribution towards accident costs suffered by pedestrians and cyclists equivalent to the total cost less insurance payments. The cost to car users of accidents caused by buses and lorries would be subtracted from this sum.[29] In addition, fuel taxation should cover those accident costs that are not borne by vehicle users but are met by the state.[30] Or, what is preferable where administratively possible, they should be met by a direct charge as is now proposed for those accident costs that are borne by the Health Service. In the case of car users these have been estimated by the DoE at £150 million in 1974, at 1975-6 prices.[31]

Road pricing

If the general level of fuel taxation is set in this way motorists will be charged a sum close to their long-run marginal costs, allowing for the way in which they underestimate the cost of using their cars. However, this solution does not deal with the problem of those parts of the urban road system which are already severely congested; and where the construction of relief roads would be enormously expensive because of the high price of land and would involve heavy social costs. The best way of tackling this difficulty is to use supplementary licencing in the short term and to introduce a full system of road pricing as a long-term solution. In principle, and if possible in practice, the road price should include both the cost of congestion and any social costs which are above the average level in the road pricing area and are therefore unlikely to be fully reflected in fuel taxation.

Road pricing is preferable to subsidising urban public transport because, as we have seen, this inevitably involves some loss of welfare in public transport. Road pricing is therefore a first best solution whereas subsidy is a second best solution, even if public transport remains technically efficient. If inefficiency creeps in, as it almost certainly will, subsidising becomes a third best.

It may be urged that road pricing is impracticable and that it would have an adverse effect on the poorer sections of the community. Neither of these objections appears to carry any weight. As long ago as 1964 the Smeed Committee showed that there were a number of ways in which road pricing could be implemented; and in 1974 a GLC Steering Group, containing members of the DoE and the Metropolitan Police, which investigated the practicability of establishing a system of supplementary licencing for central London, showed that it was both practicable and desirable.[32] Information on the incomes of those who travel into the proposed supplementary licencing area is provided by the Greater London Transportation Survey of 1971-72 which covered those who lived within the GLC's boundaries and in the surrounding built-up areas. It suggested that, apart from the poorest households, each income group accounted for about the same proportion of aggregate income as it did of drivers' journeys into the supplementary licencing area. For instance the top 4.7 per cent of households, with incomes of over £5,000, were responsible for 18.9 per cent of the trips and accounted for something like 18 per cent of total household income.[33] However the bottom 21.7 per cent of households, earning less than £1,000, with about 6 per cent of all household income, made only 2.5 per cent of driver trips. This suggests that supplementary licencing would be akin to a proportional income tax, except that it would bear less heavily on those with very low incomes. Whether the overall effect would be redistributive or regressive would obviously depend on how the revenue was spent, but the licences themselves would probably be slightly progressive.

Living without subsidies

In *The Rail Problem* John Dodgson and I argued that British Rail could be made self-financing and showed in detail how this could be achieved. It was found that BR has considerable scope for saving manpower, should be able to increase revenue by selective increases in passenger and freight charges and needs considerably less capital expenditure than it is planning. In subsequent evidence to the Select Committee on Nationalised Industries we re-examined our conclusions in the light of recent developments, the latest information and BR's comments on our findings.[34] We see no reason to change our view that BR can be made to pay its way without the need for drastic surgery. This does not mean that passenger services should be retained where they are grossly unprofitable and carry very little traffic. An examination of the available cost-benefit studies, and the costs and revenues of those of BR's services that used to be grant aided, reveals that a considerable number outside London and the principal conurbations have no social justification.[35]

Although bus operators have less scope than BR to save manpower, some improvement in their efficiency should be possible. International comparisons suggest that London Transport's buses are over-staffed, there appear to be significant differences in efficiency between undertakings and the number of supporting workers seems very high in relation to the number of drivers.[36] If, as proposed, taxation on petrol is substantially increased and supplementary licencing is introduced, some traffic will be diverted from private to public transport. This should prevent load factors from dropping and even lead to some increase. Supplementary licencing should also assist bus operators by raising speeds at peak periods and hence improving the utilisation of crews and vehicles.[37] As we have seen, the demand for bus travel appears to be very inelastic, and the introduction of supplementary licencing in central London and some provincial cities would enable fares to be raised without loss of traffic.

Although buses would no longer be subsidised from the rates and general taxation, those local authorities that introduce supplementary licencing could be permitted to devote the revenue to supporting bus and rail services that would otherwise have to be withdrawn. The solution is not ideal but it would give some much needed encouragement to the introduction of road pricing, the financial assistance for public transport would not be open ended, and there is a welfare case for maintaining some unprofitable services. It is undesirable that they should be closed where their costs are smaller than the revenue that would be earned if every passenger were charged as much as he was prepared to pay. I have discussed this argument in detail elsewhere but it is almost self-evident that it is worth providing something which, although it cannot be produced at a profit, is valued so highly by consumers that what they are individually prepared to pay exceeds its costs of production.[38]

The question remains whether it will be possible to make bus services pay their way outside the major conurbations. Fortunately their financial plight is considerably less serious than that of London Transport and the Passenger Transport Executives. As we have seen, the National Bus Company and the Scottish Transport Group had a relatively modest resource deficit in 1975 when their costs, both current and capital, exceeded their commercial revenue by 22 per cent. Moreover if that part of their expenditure which was covered by bus fuel grants is ignored the figure is reduced to 19 per cent. It should not be impossible to bridge this gap by, for instance, adopting a more flexible system of pricing and providing services that are better adjusted to need. At present, because of the way in which the licencing system operates, bus undertakings tend to make a uniform charge for journeys of a given distance based upon their average costs. It should be possible to improve profitability by raising fares when and where demand is inelastic and by cutting them if it is elastic.[39] Moreover the licencing system appears to have led to an over emphasis on conventional stage services. In rural areas these are not always what is required. For instance when in 1971 Western National withdrew its unprofitable service from Bude to Launceston a local firm was able to introduce a fast and comfortable service from Bude to Plymouth, albeit one that is considerably less frequent.[40]

There may also be scope to improve the utilisation of buses and raise the productivity of staff. There is a lesson to be learned from the small private operators who keep their costs down by their flexible use of staff and by purchasing second-hand vehicles.[41]   The Bude firm claims to have replaced 80 per cent of Western National's services using two men instead of 22 and its vehicles are scheduled more tightly.[42] Moreover Professor Graham Rees and Mr Richard Wragg, when investigating transport in rural Wales, found that the costs per vehicle mile of small private operators were significantly lower than those of the National Bus Company as represented by Crosville. Here again the present licencing system is probably to blame because of the way in which it has protected existing operators even if they are less than fully efficient.

If the National and Scottish bus groups, which account for the great bulk of rural stage services, withdrew those that are unprofitable these might be partly replaced by private operators. This is suggested both by past experience and by the fact that private operators often have vehicles that are under-used because they are largely employed on school and other contract work, which is restricted to particular times of the day.[43] They will therefore sometimes be able, once routes have been relinquished by the national bus companies, to operate an off-peak service. But this will not always be possible or profitable and it will obviously be limited to particular parts of the day. Moreover the maintenance of conventional bus services will become more and more difficult as car ownership spreads and patronage declines, although in some cases it may be possible to resort to unorthodox methods of operation such as the use of unpaid volunteer drivers. Experimental services of this type have recently been introduced in remote areas in Norfolk, Clwyd and Suffolk and are working very successfully.[44]

It seems likely, however, that in many places it will prove impossible to maintain a bus service of any shape or sort. The answer would appear to be local community action and legal changes to facilitate car sharing and the provision of lifts. At present it is illegal for a passenger to pay the person who gives him a lift unless the driver holds a licence entitling him to carry fare-paying passengers. This is unfortunate because, although there is considerable willingness to give lifts in rural areas, those without cars seem reluctant to ask. From the surveys which were conducted in Devon and West Suffolk it appears that more would ask if they could pay the driver something.[45]

This would only be an extension of what already happens. As the official study group in rural transport in Devon commented:

> The absence of buses is compensated for by increased use of cars and by getting lifts. A greater proportion of people in the poorly served areas get regular daily lifts. There was also a greater willingness among drivers in these areas to offer lifts. . . . Where there is no bus service the alternative is to try to build the solution around the use of the car. More people in our survey areas took lifts than went by stage bus. The number of car journeys made means that there is scope for more lifts in such areas as these, if ways

can be found to match the readiness to give lifts with the requirement of those without cars.[46]

What is wanted, as the study group on West Suffolk observed, is the establishment, in each village where public transport is inadequate, of a rudimentary clearing house system to bring those who need lifts and those who are willing to provide them into contact.[47] The Norfolk bus experiment, which is organised by a local committee and has found a dedicated secretary, shows that community action of this type is by no means out of the question.[48] Where a journey of some importance needs to be made and no lift is available, one can probably be specially arranged. A number of volunteer bodies already help in cases of transport hardship and provide certain services to hospitals.[49] Drivers sometimes receive a mileage allowance to cover their costs and this would seem a much better use of public funds than the indiscriminate subsidy of buses that may not run to the right place or at the right time.

Conclusion

Subsidies have increased, are increasing and ought to be diminished. Rail experience shows that they lead to inefficient use of manpower and wasteful investment. Theoretical analysis suggests that even if subsidies are largely devoted to cutting fares they are likely to reduce the welfare of the community, and in practice there is unlikely to be any substantial transfer of traffic from car to public transport. Rail support benefits the most affluent sections of the community and although bus subsidies probably have an equalising effect on the distribution of income it is preferable to redistribute by other more direct means. Cash benefits would have a greater impact and their recipients would be able to spend the money in the way that yields them the greatest satisfaction. Concessionary schemes should be withdrawn but bus fares should be lower at off-peak periods than during the rush hour in order to help fill empty seats.

Motorists do not appear to be paying enough in fuel taxation to cover their share of public expenditure on roads. Moreover they underestimate the cost of running their cars and do not meet the full cost of the accidents they cause. There should therefore be a considerable increase in fuel taxation, although car tax and car licences ought to be abolished. In central London and other places where congestion is serious supplementary licencing should be introduced as a step towards road pricing.

These measures will help transport operators to pay their way, if only by enabling them to raise their fares without losing traffic. BR can be made self-financing by raising charges, saving manpower and restricting investment, and bus undertakings can raise fares and probably have some scope for greater efficiency. In rural areas bus undertakings could, if the licencing system were reformed, charge what the market would bear, adjust their services more closely to customers' requirements and maintain off-peak services with vehicles that are not being used. Rural services are bound to contract but the needs of those without cars can, for instance, be met through local schemes to put those requiring transport in touch with those willing to give lifts.

Subsidies have the drawback that they tend to escalate partly because they weaken operators' cost control and partly owing to pressure from transport users for low fares, from trade unions on job protection and from those who believe in public transport as an act of faith. The obligation to cover costs is a financial Hadrian's Wall and once it has been decisively breached by a subsidy there is no obvious point at which a stand can be made. I therefore conclude that subsidies to public transport should be eliminated as quickly as possible and that operators should be expected to pay their way.

1. DoE, *Transport Policy : A Consultation Document,* Vol. 2, p. 112.
2. Public Expenditure to 1979-80, Cmnd. 6393, HMSO, 1976, Tables 2.5, 2.6.
3. Richard Pryke and John Dodgson, Memorandum of Evidence on British Rail, in Select Committee on Nationalised Industries, Minutes of Evidence, 18 May 1976, pp. 17, 18.
4. Here and in subsequent paragraphs I have drawn on R. W. S. Pryke and J. S. Dodgson, *The Rail Problem,* Martin Robertson, 1975, Chapter 1.
5. Stewart Joy, *The Train that Ran Away,* Ian Allan, 1973, p. 93.
6. British Railways Board, *Annual Report and Accounts 1974,* pp. 11, 49, 1975, p. 57; British Railways Board, *Transport Policy: An Opportunity for Change,* pp. 57-58; DoE, op. cit., Vol. 1, pp. 50, 53.
7. British Railways Board, *Transport Policy: An Opportunity for Change,* pp. 60-61; R. W. S. Pryke and J. S. Dodgson, op. cit., pp. 136-37.
8. Ibid., Chapter 7; Richard Pryke and John Dodgson, op. cit., pp. 16, 29, 30.
9. Union Pacific Railroad Company, *A Brief Survey of Railroads of Selected Industrial Countries,* 1975, pp. 60, 71, 78, 89.
10. If the undertaking is operating under conditions of increasing cost, inefficiency will, other things equal, result in a larger welfare loss; while if long-run marginal costs are declining and inefficiency can be avoided, or kept to modest proportions, subsidy will result in a welfare gain. This is the classical argument for subsidising railways, which, when starting de novo, have declining long-run marginal costs. However, subsidy is unnecessary if it is possible for the railway to practise price discrimination. Moreover, in practice BR almost certainly charges much less than its long-run marginal cost and any significant expansion in its output would involve heavy investment and a sharp rise in its capital charges per unit of output.
11. If it is already unprofitable, or failing to meet its long-run marginal costs, the welfare loss will be even larger.
12. Herbert J. Baum, Free Public Transport, *Journal of Transport Economics and Policy,* Vol. VII, No. 1, January 1973, pp. 8-10.
13. Central Policy Review Staff, *The Future of the British Car Industry,* HMSO, 1975, p. 32.
14. DoE, op. cit., Vol. 2, pp. 67, 68.
15. Herbert J. Baum, op. cit., pp. 4, 5; J. M. Thompson, An Evaluation of the Two Proposals for Traffic Restraint in Central London, *Journal of the Royal Statistical Society,* Series A, 1967, p. 348.
16. Department of Employment, *Family Expenditure Survey : Report for 1971,* HMSO, 1972, Table 1.
17. DoE, op. cit., Vol. 2, p. 41; information from DoE. The figures are for those households which had the highest incomes after allowance had been made for differences in household composition; the incomes of households with children had, for instance, been deflated and the incomes of single persons grossed up.
18. Ibid., p. 34. These figures also allow for differences in household composition. Those non-pensioner households included in the richest 20 per cent comprised 24 per cent of all non-pensioner households, while those in the bottom 40 per cent accounted for 30 per cent.
19. Ibid., p. 39.

20. Ralph Turvey, *Economic Analysis and Public Enterprises,* Allen and Unwin, 1971, p. 83, 84; W. J. Tyson, The Peak in Road Passenger Transport, *Journal of Transport Economics and Policy,* Vol. VI, No. 1, January 1972, pp. 79-82.

21. PEP, *Personal Mobility and Transport Policy,* Broadsheet No. 542, June 1973, p.16.

22. This does not mean that I disagree with the provision of health and education in kind, because here special considerations apply.

23. DoE, op. cit., Vol. 2, p. 112.

24. Idem.

25. PEP, op. cit., p. 25; Penelope M. Williams, Low Fares and the Urban Transport Problem, *Urban Studies,* Vol. 6, No. 1, February 1969, pp. 84, 85.

26. Expenditure in 1974 at current prices was converted with the retail price index (*Department of Employment Gazette,* May 1976, Table 132).

27. Central Statistical Office, *National Income and Expenditure 1964-74,* HMSO, 1975, Table 29; Department of Energy, *Digest of United Kingdom Energy Statistics 1975,* HMSO, 1975, Table 44.

28. DoE, op. cit., Vol. 2, p. 118.

29. This may seem unfair because pedestrians and cyclists are sometimes to blame for accidents. However, pricing decisions should, I believe, be made on efficiency grounds and considerations about equity and distribution of income should be left to the courts, etc.

30. In principle therefore fuel taxation should also include those residual costs that are borne by those who are not involved in the accident, e.g. the grief suffered by those members of the family who are not in the car when its occupants are killed.

31. DoE, op. cit., p. 120. This figure is likely to be an under-estimate because it excludes those costs that are recovered through national insurance contributions. Since these have to be paid they cannot have any effect on car use and are therefore irrelevant.

32. Ministry of Transport, *Road Pricing: The Economic and Technical Possibilities,* HMSO, 1964; Greater London Council, *A Study of Supplementary Licensing,* 1974.

33. Unpublished tabulations. The only available income data are the proportion of households in each of nine income brackets (Greater London Transportation Survey Note 120). It was assumed that the average income for each cell was the mid-point of the bracket, that households with incomes of less than £500 per annum earned £430, and that those with incomes of more than £5,000 earned £8,525: the average for income units in London and the South East (Board of Inland Revenue, *Inland Revenue Statistics 1974,* HMSO, 1974, Table 71).

34. Richard Pryke and John Dodgson, op. cit., pp. 23-37, 54.

35. Ibid., pp. 38-41.

36. Edward Smith, An Economic Comparison of Urban Railways and Express Bus Services, *Journal of Transport Economics and Policy,* Vol. VII, No. 1, January 1973, p. 24; DoE, *Passenger Transport in Great Britain 1973,* Table 28.

37. Greater London Council, op. cit., p. 74.

38. R. W. S. Pryke and J. S. Dodgson, op. cit., pp. 187-92.

39. John Hibbs, *The Bus and Coach Industry: Its Economics and Organisation,* Dent, 1975, pp. 80, 81, 132, 133, 165.

40. Keith Turns, *The Independent Bus,* David and Charles, 1974, pp. 182-84.

41. DoE, *Rural Transport in Devon,* p. 12; *Rural Transport in West Suffolk,* p. 5.

42. Keith Turns, op. cit., pp. 183, 184; Graham Rees and Richard Wragg, *A Study of the Passenger Transport Needs of Rural Wales,* Welsh Council, 1975, pp. 21-24.

43. Keith Turns, op. cit., pp. 140, 141, 183; DoE, *Rural Transport in Devon,* pp. 4, 5, 12; *Passenger Transport in Great Britain,* 1973, Table 27.

44. *Coaching Journal,* June 1976, pp. 47, 48.

45. DoE, *Rural Transport in West Suffolk,* pp. 13, 24, 27.

46. DoE, *Rural Transport in Devon,* pp. 9, 14.

47. DoE, *Rural Transport in West Suffolk,* pp. 14, 16.

48. *Coaching Journal,* June 1976, p.48.

49. DoE, op. cit., p. 14, *Rural Transport in Devon,* p. 14.

TRANSPORT AND THE ENVIRONMENT

Peter Hills*

Introduction

In confronting a very wide subject, this paper will be confined to four main tasks:

(i)   to describe in broad terms the evolution in Britain of public concern for the environment in relation to transport;

(ii)   to discuss the response by both politicians and professional transportation analysts to this growing awareness of environmental issues;

(iii)   to consider the effect this response has had on the techniques employed for assessing the impact of transport policies on the environment; and

(iv)   to set down the implications both for future policy and research that arise not only from the inadequacies of present techniques but also from the imbalances of perception by the public at large as to the nature and potency of threats to their environment.

The third of these, namely the burgeoning of new techniques, need not detain us; as (with one or two notable exceptions) almost no new techniques have so far emerged to deal with the other than strictly economic aspects of environmental evaluation. For the most part, 'environment' has rated a few platitudinous paragraphs towards the end of most consultants' reports (the end of a study being the conventionally agreed place for evaluation). The exceptions that deserve to be mentioned are the studies of Coventry,[1] Edinburgh[2] and Bristol,[3] where, in each case, attempts have been made to develop techniques more appropriate to the nature of the task.

Evolution of public awareness and concern

Legislation, particularly of a restrictive kind, can only be sustained in a democratic society by the widespread pressure of public opinion. Likewise, requirements of a non-statutory kind also require wide popular backing if they are to be instituted and maintained. The necessary level of awareness and concern

* Assistant Director of Research, Institute for Transport Studies, University of Leeds

for the environment has arisen only in very recent years and may yet prove to be founded, at least partially, on caprice. Certainly, before World War II, there was little evidence of any appreciable public awareness or concern for the environment. Motorised transport was still a novelty. Commercial vehicles, for example, were few in number (scarcely 500,000 in 1939 compared with nearly two million now) and private vehicles were strongly identified with privilege and success in a relatively hierarchical society. Newsreels of the period reflect the 'glamour' attaching to speed and power whilst the accident figures reflect a callous disregard for this most tangible of environmental hazards. Nevertheless, with a steadily rising vehicle ownership, the development of roads was seen as wholly consonant with, and an important contribution to, the community's well-being. The only significant legislation relating to traffic and the environment of which I am aware in this period was the Road Traffic Act (1934), which introduced *inter alia* blanket speed limits in urban areas to deal with the appalling accident rate, and the so-called 'ribbon development' controls of 1936, which sought to inhibit the effects on land use of increasing levels of car use both for commuting and recreation. Both pieces of legislation were strikingly successful in their separate ways; but both were introduced as panic measures and their effects were much more widespread and long-lived than their sponsors could naïvely have predicted. The lesson for us, in any round of environmental legislation we may indulge in now, is that blanket restrictions may be effective in the single dimension to which they are applied but they often impose distortions (socially as well as economically) that can hamper future development.

In the postwar period, up to the late 1950s, extremely scant resources were devoted to development of transport systems with precedence being given overwhelmingly to housing and urban reconstruction. The promise of railway modernisation, following nationalisation in 1947, did not materialise for ten years; and by 1955 expenditure on road construction had disappeared from the list of Civil Estimates. The Minister of Transport was not even accorded Cabinet rank. Even the rapid growth of air traffic after the War was accommodated on former military airfields without the potential threat to the environment being recognised. The degree of public acquiescence in the designation (in 1946) of Heathrow as London's major airport is unimaginable now. Once again, during a period of resurgent prosperity, the rising level of transport activity was widely seen as indicative of social advance. Concern still centred upon traffic accidents but, without major investment projects to act as catalysts, little or no public reaction was expressed against the steady erosion of the environment as traffic levels increased.

Nevertheless, the pressures leading to subsequent awareness and concern were mounting – the onset of mass car ownership (new registrations from 1959 onwards were persistently above one million per year, exceeding two million per year for the first time in 1972); the widespread introduction of jet airliners (the exceedingly noisy B707, for example, was in service in late 1957) and growing congestion at existing airports; the chronic deficits on the railways (despite capital write-off on the Modernisation programme) with its traffic increasingly undermined by competition from road transport; and considerable expansion of the trunk road and inter-urban motorway system under way (the first stretch of motorway opened to traffic in 1958).

Concern expressed by the few in the early 1960s (notably the Wilson Committee[4] reporting on the noise problem in 1963 and the Buchanan Report[5] published in the same year, which demonstrated the much wider implications for the environment of traffic growth) was not reflected in public awareness at the time and was actively discounted by much professional opinion despite the official endorsement these reports received. The bursting of the pressures to form a wave of popular reaction against the environmental consequences of major transport investment schemes did not really occur until the late 1960s. Reaction centred on two issues: (a) the effects of comprehensive urban renewal and (b) the effects of urban motorway construction. Both of these issues were crucial to the accommodation of a high level of car use in urban areas without undue sacrifice of environmental conditions. Buchanan[6] spelled out the need for public acceptance of these as a precondition, without which, he argued, severe traffic restraint would be inevitable. As I see it, the public have largely rejected the principles of comprehensive redevelopment (with its associated costs and disruptions) and are only now beginning to accept the concomitant discipline of traffic restraint. Unless a substantial back-wave is generated during the next phase of real income growth and prosperity, the transformation of social attitudes towards urban conservation may be seen as the lasting tribute to the strenuous work of the environmental lobby over the last six or eight years. The twin high points can already be seen in the outcome of the GLDP inquiry and the overturning of the Roskill Commission's inquiry.[7] In each case, the explicit recognition of the environmental effects played a decisive rôle in influencing the result. Subsequently the pressure that brought this influence to bear appears to have slackened, having diffused into much wider areas of concern – for example, the so-called energy crisis, price-inflation and the need to restrict Government expenditure, the social consequence of unemployment, and so on. Even the strictest environmentalists seem bemused now with speculation as to the effect of continued economic growth on the ecosystem – a subject peculiarly deficient in objective evidence or established relationships.

To explain where this remarkable social evolution leaves us at present and what it signifies for the future of both policy and research we have to examine the responses of two important groups: namely the politicians charged with the task of taking decisions on planning and transport matters and the professionals whose jobs it is to advise them. The word sketch which follows is, of necessity, generalised but it may serve to explain the present predicament and provide a basis for discussion.

Responses by professionals and politicians

With hindsight, it is fair to say that (in general) both politicians and pro-fessionals were knocked off balance by the momentum which the environmental wave acquired during the late 1960s. Those few academics and practitioners who had foreseen it (some of whom even promoted it) were for the most part overtaken by it; ironically, Buchanan, although a consistent advocate of environ-mental standards, found himself engulfed as, successively, plans for Bath, Cardiff and Edinburgh were thrown out. Few of the major transportation plans have escaped and those that have (notably Glasgow and the West Midlands) are now faced with cutbacks in capital expenditure, which may well emasculate their grandiose highway proposals.

Not surprisingly, the politicians tended to be the ones to regain their footing first; at least at the local government level – owing, no doubt, to their greater sensitivity to shifts in political opinion and to their closer proximity to the grass roots where the most profound shifts were occurring. Repeatedly in recent years – often following a change in the ruling majority, as Grant[8] has shown in relation to Nottingham, Southampton and Portsmouth – city councils have reversed decisions already made in favour of urban motorway plans. In many cases, this has been a result of 'lightning conversions' by local politicians who had previously acquiesed in the plan!

As far as policy makers (at the national level) and professionals were con-cerned, the responses followed almost wholly in the wake of public concern – I would even venture to suggest that a not insignificant minority were antagonistic to the environmental cause or at least optimistic that in time the wave would pass. In great part, this response reflected: (a) the lack of any adequate frame-work of analysis of environmental impact, which, in any case, would probably have muddied the 'technical purity' of the planning process; and (b) the essen-tially 'trans-disciplinary' nature of the issues themselves, which meant that pro-fessionally (and departmentally) speaking they were the responsibility of no one. The rigid disciplinary lines on which we had all been brought up prevented us from perceiving the new dimensions of the problem and from adjusting properly to them. Of all those disciplines involved, this was probably most true of engineers who at the time were, and perhaps still are, disproportionately represented in transportation study teams. Certainly the belief that the transport-ation planning process is a wholly technical matter has been a particularly enduring one. And yet, in recent years, many transportation plans (for small towns as well as large) have been thrown out not for reasons of technical incompetence but for the assumption within them of implicit social and political values — particularly in relation to the environment.

That this is *now* widely realised is clear from the Report of the Select Committee of the House of Commons[9] on Urban Transport Planning. In itself, a remarkably unequivocal statement of professional contrition — but it did not appear in public until late 1972.

Evidence to support the contention that professionals and central policy makers have been trailing in this respect may be seen in the surprising lack of legislation and the dearth of thorough-going research sponsored over the last ten years.

The most vigorous initiative at the centre probably came with the appointment of the Urban Motorways Committee[10] whose recommendations may perversely have clouded the problem. The suggestion, for instance, that much wider powers for comprehensive redevelopment be invoked in order to 'fit motorways into' the urban environment in a less intrusive way invites authorities to jump out of the frying-pan . . . Clearly, the enduring legacy of the UMC report will be their noise level standard (based on the 18-hour L_{10} index) which, although scrupulously presented as a 'compensation threshold', has inevitably been seized upon as a design standard and applied as such. The danger is that this process may be repeated for a whole host of arbitrarily defined environmental hazards without sufficient allowance being given for their built-in cost implications, their perceived importance as hazards by those actually exposed to them or to their interdependence as variables.

Admittedly the Buchanan Report[11] urged the adoption of objectively specified environmental standards, but subsequent research (notably by Crompton and Gilbert[12] at Imperial College and JURUE[13] at Birmingham) has shown how this basic 'standards' approach can be elaborated and made more flexible — the studies of Edinburgh,[14] Bath[15] and Hammersmith[16] are good examples. But these are almost lone pioneering efforts: in the 13 years since the Buchanan Report, more importantly in the last six to eight years of intense public concern, where have been the massive concentrations of effort and the wholesale injection of research funds to tackle these issues? The work of Lassière and Bowers at the DoE must be acknowledged — especially their comprehensive tour-de-force presented to the ECMT 18th Round Table[17] in April 1972. Likewise, Dawson and others[18] at TRRL have worked patiently (if rather speculatively) at testing simulated impacts on the environment; and, rumour has it, another tome from Lassière is shortly to emerge. Comment should also be made on the sporadic attempts to determine stable average values for environmental compensation and direct measures of householders' surplus. Probably the most concerted of these attempts were made in connection with the Roskill Inquiry.[19] Although important and occasionally revealing, these trade-off studies have always been hampered by lack of control over fundamental variables (eg. locational effects, employment opportunities etc.) to the extent sometimes of producing perverse results. The difficulties, inherent in direct valuation based upon real world consumers' behaviour, have led to various ways of simulating the trade-off between environmental goods under conditions of budget limitation (the work of Social and Community Planning Research[20] is most notable here).

But even summing all these individual efforts, financed in a parsimonious and ill-coordinated way, no one could claim that the scale of effort has been sufficient to match the level of public concern. And yet, ironically we may now be well placed to develop the most appropriate policies and to pursue them in an intelligent and enlightened way. For we have at least avoided panic legislation and pressure for this, although it persists, is declining. We have avoided so far the erection of a panoply of rigid and (necessarily) arbitrary standards with the single exception of noise – but this, to be fair, is an aspect of environmental intrusion where the need for regulation is most widely accepted. In so far as it is not a contradiction in terms, we have also avoided panic research.

Implications for policy and research

This gives us an opportunity which must be secured in the next few years, if it is not to be lost for a generation. The profile of this opportunity may be characterised thus:

Now that the intensity of public *concern* has waned, but a much higher level of *awareness* remains, the scope for suitable balanced legislation is improving rapidly.

Now that investment resources are becoming relatively scarce, the temptation to introduce environmental standards that are *not* reflective of weighted social preferences (or, ideally, consensus social values) can be more easily resisted. For instance, the adoption of pollution control devices on cars to meet the high standards demanded by environmentalists would carry in many cases the penalty of increased fuel consumption to the dismay of conservationists.

Now that the hyperbole of doom-prediction based upon highly plausible, but often fatally quantitative, arguments has died down, policy makers can set about the task of identifying the issues of real perceived importance. Where clinical hazards exist that are unperceived, measures can be devised for environmental protection based upon consistent estimates of risk and consistent values applied to the maintenance of health and preservation of life (or, more strictly, the postponement of death). For example, there are enormous differences in the levels of risk regarded as tolerable by the community not only for pedestrians as opposed to vehicle occupants but also between the various modes of transport. This is just one of many areas of interaction between environmental protection policies and the distribution of resources within the transport sector.

For the public concern generated by (for example) the Moorgate Tube crash to be offset by an awareness of the numbers of dead and injured on the roads over the period of its press coverage and of the comparable levels of risk that attend elderly pedestrians or child cyclists every day predicates much wider dissemination of objectively relevant data. The neglect of public information on matters relating to the environment has contributed a great deal to the widespread imbalances of perception by the community at large as to the relative seriousness of the various threats to the environment. The latest example of this is to be seen in the current 'asbestosis' scares. For even as he reads of the hidden dangers of drilling a few holes in the asbestos walls of his garden shed, a commuter may be breathing in air laden with dust from the brake linings of an Underground train. The crucial implication for policy lies in the relative cost and inflexibility of legislation. By raising levels of awareness through public information the need for legislation could be substantially reduced.

However, to progress in this direction with policy presupposes that information of sufficient comprehensiveness and accuracy exists. This, in turn, relies vitally on a well directed and well coordinated research effort of which the overall aims should be:

to pursue the identification of the relative importance of environmental factors as perceived by individuals actually subject to the prevailing conditions – the rank order of these factors may well vary as between different person types and activities;

to develop and refine techniques of measuring *subjective* responses which begin to match our technical skills in the *physical* measurement of environmental conditions themselves;

to devise an altogether more appropriate method of evaluation which does more than merely regard environmental costs and benefits as elements in some crude economic trade-off mechanism;

to reflect the essentially trans-disciplinary nature of environmental studies in relation to transport. (Our own work at Leeds University in which we have concentrated upon the effects of pedestrianisation schemes have combined the talents of economists, engineers and applied psychologists.)

Without this kind of basic research, rooted in the analysis of subjective responses to a whole range of environmental conditions, and well balanced policies, based upon the highest possible level of public awareness of environmental hazard, we may well be committed to costly and inhibiting regulations

73

which do not accord with our other social priorities. We should preserve legislation only for the most vital aspects of environmental protection. In this connection, we should view with some alarm the pressure for the preparation of Environmental Impact Statements (EIS) to become a mandatory part of the planning process, as it is now in the USA. The danger is of requiring a vast amount of detailed information to be collected, relevant only to the scheme proposed, without comparable efforts to inform people about conditions elsewhere against which the scheme should be judged. More importantly, data may be entered into the evaluation for no other reason than they were required to be collected: this can only serve to confuse and confound our genuine efforts to reach 'optimal' decisions in relation to the environment.

1. City of Coventry, *The Coventry Transportation Study,* Phase II (Chapter 7), December 1972.

2. Colin Buchanan and Partners, Indices of Environmental Conditions in Central Area Streets, in *City of Edinburgh Planning and Transportation Study,* November 1971.

3. Jamison, Mackay and Partners, *Bristol Study: Strategic Environmental Evaluation Techniques,* Part I, April 1975.

4. Wilson Committee, *Final Report on the Problem of Noise,* HMSO, July 1963.

5. Buchanan Report, *Traffic in Towns,* Ministry of Transport, HMSO, November 1963.

6. Buchanan Report, op. cit.

7. *Report of the Roskill Commission of Inquiry into the Siting of the Third London Airport,* HMSO, 1970.

8. John A. Grant, Urban Transportation and Decision Making — a comparison of three case studies in Britain, *Transportation,* Vol. 4, No. 2, June 1975.

9. *Report of the Expenditure Committee of the House of Commons on Urban Transport Planning,* HMSO, November 1972.

10. Urban Motorways Committee, *Report of Urban Project Team,* DoE, HMSO, London, 1973.

11. Buchanan Report, op. cit.

12. D. H. Crompton and D. A. M. Gilbert, in Colin Buchanan and Partners, op. cit.

13. F. E. Joyce and H. Williams, On assessing environmental impact of urban road traffic, *International Journal of Environmental Studies,* Vol 3, pp. 201-27, April 1972.

14. Colin Buchanan and Partners, op. cit.

15. Colin Buchanan and Partners, Bath and Planning and Transport Study, Commissioned by Bath City Corporation, dated December 1965.

16. Joyce and Williams, op. cit.

17. A. Lassière and P. Bowers, Studies on the Social Costs of Urban Road Transport (Noise and Pollution), *ECMT 18th Round Table on Transport Economics,* Paris, April 1972.

18. R. F. F. Dawson et al., Environmental Simulator: progress report, TRRL *Laboratory Report 659,* Crowthorne, UK, 1974.

19. Roskill Commission, op. cit.

20. G. Hoinville, *Measuring Consumer Priority, SCPR (forthcoming).*

STATISTICAL NEEDS FOR PUBLIC POLICIES FOR TRANSPORT

Ray Thomas*

Statistics are collected by organisations. That statement is almost a tautology, but some of the corollaries may not be so apparent. Official statistics reflect the nature of organisations: not necessarily the statistical needs of public policy making. Often these needs of organisations correspond with those of public policy. But this is not true of transport.

In transport the official statistics reflect operators' needs or the needs of bodies concerned with investment for specific transport modes. But it is probably more difficult in transport than in any other area to assume for any single sector, or for transport as a whole, that there is a correlation between what these statistics measure – output, or some measure derived from output – and the public interest. If car travel increases it certainly cannot be said that society is in any way better off. The increase in car travel has probably been associated with a decline in public transport services – so that some people are worse off.

Even if the volume of travel as a whole is increasing it cannot be said that society is better off. Transport is a means to an end, not something usually valued for its own sake. The fact that in cost-benefit studies even non-working time spent travelling is treated as a cost (and usually represents a substantial proportion of the total cost) indicates that on conventional assumptions the greater the volume of travel the worse off we are.

Public transport statistics

The major series of historical statistics relating to personal movement are for passenger journeys and passenger mileage. Until the 1950s this was virtually the only information available on personal travel, mainly because this was the only information on personal travel needed by public transport operators. In conjunction with the other statistics on assets, staff, vehicle movements, revenue and expenditure these statistics on journeys and mileage provided an adequate means at that time of what would nowadays be called monitoring performance.

The monopolistic position enjoyed by public transport meant, for example, that there was little need to distinguish between peak and off-peak travel. Statistics relating to the timing of journeys must have been collected by many

* Senior Lecturer in Economics, Open University

operators, but few of these data found their way into published sources. Cheap season tickets on the railways, for example, were originally introduced with the objective of lengthening journeys to work. They were offered at prices substantially below ordinary fare levels because it was assumed that the commuter traffic was profitable. New stations and lines were being built and the marginal cost of providing extra peak services appeared to be very low. The imbalance between peak and off-peak travel was not even seen as a problem until the growth of television viewing and car ownership seriously eroded off-peak travel.[1]

Neither were public transport operators generally interested in origin and destination data. The number of passengers on existing routes was regarded as sufficient guidance for meeting demand. In major urban areas such as London there may well have been wasteful competition between different public transport modes, and in many areas it is possible that operators missed opportunities to respond to changes in demand through the provision of new services rather than changes in existing services. But public transport operation was seen as being concerned with the provision of adequate services which could usually be defined only in terms of existing demand on established travel routes.

The lack of detail in travel statistics can be seen as one aspect of the conservative nature of the public transport industry which limited its power and ability to compete with television and the motor car. The possibilities for developing new public policies to deal with changes in the transport situation were correspondingly limited by the restriction of statistics to large aggregates of total passenger journeys or mileage. These statistics show that public transport has declined in London since the late 1940s and in most other areas by the early 1950s. It is difficult to see that these trends have any clear and simple implications for public policies. There appears to be no reason to regret the decline in passenger mileage other than the consequent decline in standards of service.

Private vehicle travel

The major historical series relating to travel by private vehicle are for the number of cars licenced and data from traffic censuses. The major purpose for collecting statistics on vehicles was originally fiscal and the first national census was carried out in 1926. The major purpose of carrying out traffic censuses was to guide investment under the administration of the road fund, and the first census was carried out on class 1 roads in 1922.[2] Neither of these series relates directly to personal travel, and the historical series for 'passenger' mileage by private vehicle is based upon estimates of vehicle mileage from traffic counts and average occupancy from travel surveys. The first estimates of the total volume of passenger mileage by private vehicle were made only after passenger mileage by private vehicle had already overtaken that mileage by public transport in the 1950s.[3]

The initial response to the growth of private vehicle use in the 1950s was to collect data on car parking. At that time even London Transport believed that its problems would be solved if parked cars did not impede its bus operations. A number of such surveys were carried out in the 1950s in central London. The new information derived from these surveys sustained for a decade or more the belief that the solution to congestion problems lay in the provision of more off-street parking spaces.

In response to the demand for major new urban road investments came the flowering of the Land Use Transportation Surveys of the 1960s – with origin and destination data, journey timings, and journey purpose for all travel involving motorised means of transport. For the first time some aspects of the complexity of urban interaction were expressed in statistical form. The richness of these data swiftly proved to be too much to handle without aggregation into 'desire lines', and it also soon became apparent that such desire lines for motorised vehicle travel could be more cheaply estimated from data on the distribution of employment, residential population and car ownership.

Indivisibilities and aggregation

The experience of the Land Use Transportation Surveys has important implications for the relationship between transport efficiency and economic efficiency. Moderately aggregate statistics, such as are expressed in the form of desire lines, point the need for new transport provision. But to deal with this aggregate demand in a way which is economic from the point of view of transport operation requires heavy investment of a very specific kind – such as the Victoria Line, or a new motorway. Economic efficiency on the other hand is usually conceived as requiring some correspondence between cost to the consumer and resource costs. The specific investment required for efficiency in transport operation reduces this correspondence. Travellers on the Victoria Line pay the same as those on other parts of the Underground system. Motorists on a motorway pay roughly the same as motorists using other roads.

There are also limitations from the point of view of public policy in the use of aggregate statistics of existing travel patterns. Catering to the demand in one part of the system can easily lead to under-utilisation of capacity in other parts of the system and thence to a decline in the facilities available in other parts of the system. The provision of a new transport facility may, of course, create a new demand. But in this case it is doubtful whether public investment should have been based upon statistics of existing demand.

The aggregate statistics show that in 1973 there was roughly four times as much travel in terms of passenger mileage by private car as by all forms of public road and rail transport. The factors which have contributed to this particular balance are well known. Car travel is costly, but for the large majority of journeys it is convenient, and for the large majority of users it is addictive. Travel by public transport is usually slightly less costly, it is rarely convenient, it is addictive only for the commuter, and it is generally only the first choice of those without access to a motor car. The possibilities of public transport competing with the motor car are almost negligible. For as long as people can afford to travel by car so will they choose to travel by car.

Two sorts of criteria are relevant to public policy formulation in this situation. First, investment to accommodate the motor car can be convincingly justified to the extent that car use fulfils needs which cannot be met by other means. In this situation some people will be better off and nobody may be worse off. Secondly, investment to accommodate the motor car should be modified by regard for those (the majority in terms of population if not in terms of households) without cars. If mobility is facilitated for one sector of society at the expense of provision for mobility of other sectors, society as a whole may be no better off and is certainly more inequitable. Operators' statistics are of very limited usefulness for policy making according to either of these criteria. Statistics of passenger journeys made by private car give no clue as to the proportion of journey purposes which might have been fulfilled by other means. The relationship between the growth of car use and the decline in public transport is complex, and involves many intervening variables. Little can be learned of this interdependence directly from statistics of passenger journeys by car and public transport.

Both these criteria on the other hand point to the need for statistics on substitutes for motorised travel, and for household or individual based data rather than operator based data. Information on alternatives to motorised travel would help to identify motorised journey purposes which could be accomplished by other means, and such statistics should make it possible to take into account some of the ways in which provision for rising car use affects provision for those without access to a car. Only household or individual based data would make it possible to identify interdependencies between transport and non-transport methods of fulfilling needs, and only household or individual based data can be used to explore manifestations of inequality in the field of mobility and accessibility.

Non-motorised movement

The most obvious alternative to motorised means of transport is walking. Neil Rubra summarised the position from the statistical point of view as follows:

> We have no figures at all for travel on foot other than to and from work at present; strangely enough it is not the practice to collect data on pedestrian movements even for town centre shopping areas, construction of bridges and underpasses, siting of bus stations, or other by-products of traffic

management schemes. The information used for planning such things is more an economic than a statistical question, but it would appear that pedestrian measurements are a pre-requisite for even the simplest cost-benefit appraisal, since without them you do not know the relative importance in numbers of people between pedestrian and motorized flows. This needs to be multiplied by the time taken for each to negotiate the system. Pedestrian time is conventionally valued at double passenger time, but vehicle operating costs would have to be allowed for: however a diversion of say 350 metres takes about four minutes to walk round, or more if there is a change of levels, compared to only half a minute in a car. It may be that some subway and overbridge systems designed with safety in mind do not confer the intended benefits because the extra distance or effort puts walkers off them. If aggregate delays are less as a result, it may be preferable for vehicles rather than pedestrians to be diverted. Extending the distances travelled by vehicles may be an increasingly extravagant use of fuel as scarcity bites, but without quantifying the alternative pedestrian delays there can be no way of knowing exactly *how* extravagant.

The exclusion of shorter journeys on foot from even those few sources that do collect pedestrian data is also hard to justify other than on grounds of convenience. If all journeys by car, and even by public transport, taking less than twenty minutes were excluded, a significant part of all transport would be omitted. Data on journey times are collected only on occasional local studies, so the proportion is unknown but it might be of the order of 40 per cent of all journeys. These problems are beyond the immediate scope of this Unit, but the fact that the basic data needed to solve them are not available for inspection is strong presumptive evidence that they have not received the attention they deserve. This has serious implications when you try to establish how far pedestrian movements incur accident risk, which is considered below (pp.116-17). The traffic surveys reported in *Highway Statistics* do not include walkers in their traffic counts.

The notes from *Road Accidents* table 11, which apply to their table 12, go into a complicated explanation of how pedestrian accidents are related to vehicle miles, since the basis on which these are calculated has recently been revised. You should understand the method used if you read it carefully. It does not correspond at all with what is done for the other modes: it is an attempt to assess how far vehicle miles by various classes of traffic are a risk to pedestrians, not how risky it is to be a pedestrian. No information has ever been collected on how far people walk (other than for the journey to work) or how long they spend doing it. Hence we cannot calculate either the accident rates per mile walked or the accident rates per hour on the road walking. This is a serious shortcoming of the data.[4]

The availability of statistics on non-motorised movement for the journey to work is relatively recent. The plans for the new town of Milton Keynes, with a projected population of a quarter of a million, were made before the results of the 1966 Census Workplace statistics were available. The plan assumed that only 10 per cent of work journeys would be made by non-motorised means of transport, and that the proportion of such journeys would be independent of the nature of the plan.[5] Both assumptions can be shown to be quite erroneous on the basis of the census data. The proportion of internal work journeys by foot and bicycle in cities of around 250,000 population is much higher than 10 per cent and varies widely. For cities of between 200-300,000 in 1966 the variation ranged from 22 per cent in Sunderland to 46 per cent in Derby and in 1971 from 21 per cent in Sunderland, Plymouth and Hull to 30 per cent in Wolverhampton.[6]

These errors are not just of academic interest because the land use plan for Milton Keynes is based upon a journey to work model, and it has only been slightly modified since its conception in those days when people believed in the millenial promise of 'universal car ownership'. The case can also be used to make the point that it usually takes a long time for new statistics to be translated into their policy implications. Milton Keynes is a good example because it seems to be the largest single public investment planned in the 1960s which has survived unscathed into the mid 1970s.

The journey to work appears to be an exceptional form of travel. Journeys to work are longer than most other major types of journey. Yet journeys to work are also made more frequently than any other common type of journey. The reason why people are prepared to travel longer distances for the journey they make most often has never been satisfactorily explained.

These exceptional features of the journey to work means that it cannot be assumed that what can be learned about pedestrian (or cycling) movement from journey to work data can be applied to other types of journeys.

So there is a large hiatus. We know that walking and cycling are recommended as being a healthy form of exercise. We know that a higher proportion of the population is able to walk than is able to use any other means of transport. We know that a significant minority of the population take pleasure in walking exceptionally long distances over rough country, and cycling exceptional distances over smooth roads, but we know virtually nothing else about the volume, or the influences on the volume, of pedestrian movement or cycling except for the constrained situation of the journey to work.

Household surveys

There seems little doubt that inequalities within society manifest themselves more strongly in matters of car ownership than in any other major activity. The

80

point can be partly illustrated through the use of Lorenz curves shown in the figure. On this measure the inequality of car ownership among households is roughly of the same degree of inequality in the distribution of wealth, the degree of inequality is much greater than for income even after taxation or to take an example from another major sector, housing space, if this is measured in terms of number of rooms.

Inequality in the distribution of cars, rooms, incomes (after tax) and wealth in 1971

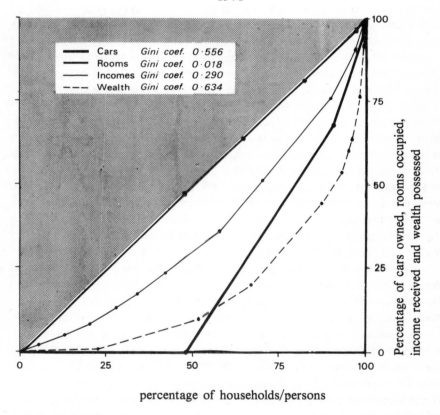

percentage of households/persons

Sources: Census of Population 1971, Inland Revenue Statistics 1971

The Lorenz curves tell only part of the story because there is also inequality within households. For most households with only one car there is only one licence holder. The housewife and the children in most of the households are dependent on the male breadwinner. For most households with two or more cars there are mostly children who often depend on the housewife to act as chauffeur. Household based data, as Mayer Hillman's studies have illustrated, are needed in order to investigate the magnitude and implications of such inequalities.

Household and individual based data are also necessary in order to establish the importance of all the non-transport substitutes for travel. It seems unlikely, for example, that lack of mobility is felt, by the household or individual concerned, to be a deprivation unless it is a reflection of lack of income.

Most of the benefits of movement can be purchased in other ways. Television delivered film into the home and reputedly had dramatic effects on evening travel as well as on cinema attendances. Not many shops nowadays appear to offer a delivery service, but the mobile shop is still evident even on streets only a few hundred yards from shopping centres. Milk is still delivered and milkmen are diversifying into other goods. Mail order still flourishes, and there are still postal deliveries six days a week. The telephone can substitute for a wide variety of potential travel movements. Residential mobility can substitute for a long journey to work.

Statistical data on many of these questions are obtainable from existing social surveys. The Family Expenditure Survey, for example, aims to record transport and communications expenditures in some detail, but does not in the usually published tables distinguish between car-owning and non-car-owning households. So that an average expenditure of £X a week for a particular type of household can mean that half the households spend £2X on motor transport and the other half nothing. FES data could and should be used to establish what difference expenditure of £2X or nothing on cars made to expenditure on, for example, telephone or postal services.

(Some would argue that examination of such relationships is a matter for research rather than statistical publications. The results of an article published in an academic journal usually take a long time to influence public policy. Government officials do not usually read academic journals. But statistics are available to a wide variety of graduate and undergraduate students and governmental officials as well as academics. The possibilities of information influencing policy quickly are much greater for statistics than research because there is such a multiplicity of channels of communication including the academic journals.)

The General Household Survey includes questions on tenure and migration, employment and changes of employment, and car ownership. But these three groups of data are not brought together in the published tables. If these data were brought together it could well throw some light on this paradoxical feature of the journey to work in being both the journey most frequently made and the longest. We already know from other surveys that people who buy a new house thereby *lengthen* their journey to work.[7] We also know that when people are

82

given the opportunity to live and work in the same area, as they are in new towns, they usually take advantage of the situation to *shorten* their journey to work.[8] Data from the GHS could be used to help make generalisations about the nature of the circumstances which added or reduced the length of journey to work and so could provide evidence on ways in which the substitution of residential for journey to work mobility might be encouraged.

It seems unlikely however that the GHS could be used in many other ways to contribute to the development of public policies for transport. The GHS is designed to show 'how various parts of life are linked' and to 'show changes in the pattern of living'.[9] But beyond the question on car ownership it includes few questions relevant to transport and encompasses batteries of questions on education and health as well as employment and housing.

New types of survey are necessary to obtain a comprehensive picture of the ways in which transport is linked to other parts of life. What is needed is FACTS. Or to put it into words, a Family Accessibility Communications and Transport Survey. This should include an inventory of communications and delivery as well as movement by members of the household.

There are analogies between such an inventory and expenditure surveys like FES and time budget studies. But the proposed FACTS would focus on personal movement and the major possible substitutes for personal movement. It would cover trips by foot and bicycle as well as by motorised means; it would cover visitors to the home as well as trips by members of the household; and it would aim to cover deliveries to the home such as the newspaper boy, the milkman and the postman. In these respects it would be much like the Land Use Transportation Surveys. But the proposed FACTS should also cover the non-transport substitutes for transport – which appear to be mainly dependent upon electronic means of communication such as the telephone, radio and television.

Data from such FACTS should help establish, for example, the substitutes for travel found by those with high incomes who choose not to be car users. It should help establish the extent to which such substitutes can be found in different types of area. Such data should make it possible to establish whether or not the degree of inequality evident in the distribution of car ownership is manifest in other areas of accessibility or mobility. And again it should help to establish the relationship between the inequalities and the type of area.

All these are the sorts of questions which ought to help shape public policies for transport at a national level. It is difficult to see how these questions can be answered without fairly regularly conducted surveys of this kind. Once every five years or so would be adequate. At a cost of, say, £200,000 a time this is not very big science.

Other diagnoses
The conclusions of this paper seem consistent with the two major reports on

transport policy published in recent years. The need for data on non-motorised movement was recognised in *Changing Directions* (The report of the Independent Commission on Transport, published in 1974) which called for social surveys to monitor consumer satisfaction.

These surveys should collect factual information about trips made, as is done at present; but instead of very large surveys at long intervals, the need is for smaller surveys conducted more frequently. These should cover journeys by foot and bicycle, which are omitted from most recent surveys, as well as journeys by motorised means. Enquiries should also be made into frustrated travel (i.e. the journeys that people would like to make, but are deterred from making by unsatisfactory conditions), unwanted travel and quality aspects of travel.[10]

But the report also recognised that personal mobility does not cover all aspects of the situation. 'The real goal is not ease of movement, but access to people and facilities. Movement is desirable only to the extent that access requires it.'[11]

The *Socialist Commentary* report 'Transport Policy' (published in 1975) in its recommendations on local transport policy is not so explicit about the need for statistics but adds the egalitarian dimension. Its first two recommendations were:

An acceptable level of mobility should be available to all potential travellers whether or not they have the use of a car, especially the old and disabled.

The relationship between transport and land use planning should be re-examined so as to reduce the need for people to travel.[12]

The emphasis in both these reports indicates the need for individual or household based statistics. The emphasis on reduction of the need for travel points to the need for statistics on other substitutes for motorised mobility.

1. For a discussion of the growth in the imbalance between peak and off-peak travel, with estimates for the period 1951-67 for London Transport, see PEP, *Journeys to Work*, Planning No. 504, November 1968.
2. For an account of prewar sources see Frederick A. A. Menzler, Rail and Road, in M.G. Kendal (ed.) *Sources and Nature of the Statistics of the United Kingdom*, Vol. I, Oliver and Boyd, 1952, pp. 279-302.
3. *The Report from the Select Committee on Nationalised Industries, British Railways,* 1960, includes one of the earliest estimates. In a paper submitted by the British Transport Commission on the position of British Railways in the transport industry of the country in 1958, it says: 'Passenger miles by private motor car and motor-cycle are estimated to be of the order of 50,000 mil-

lion' (*Report*, p 335). The current estimate for private transport in 1958 is 73,000 million passenger miles.
4. Neil Rubra, *Transport and Communication.* D291, Unit 13, Open University Press, 1975, pp. 82 and 116. (This book was written as part of a course on statistical sources.)
5. Milton Keynes Development Corporation, *The Plan for Milton. Keynes Technical Supplement No. 7, Volume 2, Transportation,* Milton Keynes Development Corporation, 1970.
6. Censuses of Population for 1966 and 1971, *Workplace Tables.*
7. See Harry Grace, Family Residential Mobility and Urban Growth, in Peter Hall (ed.), *The Containment of Urban England,* Allen and Unwin, 1972, Vol. II, pp.156-8.

84

8. Priority in housing in new towns is given to those who obtain a job in the town, and the ratio of the number of local journeys to work (i.e. living and working in the area) to the number of .commuting journeys (i.e. residents working outside and persons employed in the town resident outside) is exceptionally high in most of the new towns. See PEP, *London's New Towns,* Planning No. 510. April. 1969.

9. Office of Population Censuses and Surveys, *General Household Survey — Introductory Report,* HMSO, 1973, p. A51.
10. Independent Commission on Transport, *Changing Directions,* Coronet Books, 1974, p.197.
11. Ibid., p. 260.
12. Transport Policy — The Report of a Study Group, *Socialist Commentary,* April 1975, pp. 12 and 21.